THINGS UNSEEN

MARK BUCHANAN

Multnomah®Publishers *Sisters, Oregon*

THINGS UNSEEN
published by Multnomah Publishers, Inc.

Published in association with the literary agency of Ann Spangler and
Associates, 6560 Viewpoint Drive NE, Belmont, Michigan 49306

© 2002 by Mark Buchanan

International Standard Book Number: 0-7394-2367-0

Cover image by Frans Lemmens/Getty Images

Unless otherwise indicated, Scripture quotations are from:
The Holy Bible, New International Version © 1973, 1984 by International Bible
Society, used by permission of Zondervan Publishing House.

Multnomah is a trademark of Multnomah Publishers, Inc.,
and is registered in the U.S. Patent and Trademark Office.
The colophon is a trademark of Multnomah Publishers, Inc.

Printed in the United States of America

For information:
MULTNOMAH PUBLISHERS, INC.
POST OFFICE BOX 1720
SISTERS, OREGON 97759

I dedicate this book to all the saints,
known and unknown,
loved and hated,
past, present, and future,
who have lived their lives heaven-bent,
joyful in the Things Unseen.

CONTENTS

PART IV

HEAVEN-BENT: LIVING IN LIGHT OF FOREVER

THE BIG FIX

I'm dying.

Sometimes I forget that.

Don't misunderstand: I am not, at present, suffering from a terminal illness or a mortal wound. I have no virus breeding, thick and septic, in my bloodstream, no genetic disease swarming, swift and capricious, in my flesh. I am not, to my knowledge, dying soon.

But I am, as the apostle Paul puts it, "outwardly wasting away" (see 2 Corinthians 4:16). That's what I sometimes forget: my mortality, my frailty, my life's brevity. *I will be the exception,* I think, the one who evades death at each turn, slips its every snare, snatches hold of Elijah's chariot or Enoch's robe and, whisked into the wild blue yonder, remains unscathed by the grim reaper's scythe.

But that's laughable: I'm dying, and you're dying, and that's that.

Is there a way to remember this and not be consumed by it? Can I live life to the full when life is often not full—when it's many times broken, empty, scattered, pain-filled, when its beauties are so transitory, its pleasures so vaporous, its hard luck so tenacious? Must I, with all the trouble I'm already in, also remember that I'm dying?

Yes.

And no.

That's what this book is about: the yes and the no.

This book is about heaven, and yet not. It is about our longing for heaven, our instinct for it. It is about eternity in our hearts. It is about the groaning inside us that is both an acknowledgment of and a protest against death, and at the same time a cry for something else, for that which is beyond the grave, stronger and larger than it, more enduring. It is about our yearning for Things Unseen. It is about wanting heaven.

We groan waiting for it. Words cannot express these groans—that's why we groan—but I've set out to lay this yearning down in words anyway, to map the wild rough terrain of our everlasting desire and our desire for the everlasting. I've ventured to name the Things Unseen. And I've attempted to train us in skills for fixing our eyes on them—the unseen realities—so that we do not lose heart.

Not that I wish the groaning to cease. My hope, indeed, is that it deepens. My hope is that we learn to join our groaning, pitch for pitch and rhythm for rhythm, to the groaning of all creation—earth and sky, waterfall and water buffalo, chickadee and katydid, stone and tree—to all things as they wait for the sons of God to be revealed (see

Romans 8:22). Groaning is creation's song, the blues of the cosmos, and we're to hum its melody and take up its chorus.

So this is a book not about heaven, but about heavenly-mindedness. It's about how the *hope* of heaven inspires and sustains passion and purpose in this life and on this earth. And it's about learning the biblical lexicon and discipline for bringing heaven near—for fixing our hearts and our minds on things above.

We're heaven-bent. I mean by that a number of things: that our hearts have an inner tilt upward, that the grain of our souls leans heavenward, that in Christ we have a sure destination, which powers larger than ourselves carry us toward. I mean it in contrast to being hell-bent. But before any of that, I mean that we're all cockeyed, bent out of shape, with missing heaven. And we miss it in both senses of the word: We wish for it, yet go astray of it. We have a hunger for things above, but our skill for filling that hunger has atrophied. We're like a lapcat—still with the instinct for catching mice, but lacking the reflexes—whose pampered existence has made it slow and lazy, inept at stalking, clumsy at pouncing. It rarely catches its prey, if even it stirs to notice the prey in its midst. We're like that with heaven: We long for it, but we've lost the tautness and alertness, the agility and quickness, to satisfy the longing. We've grown lethargic. We've become so earthly-minded we're of no heavenly good.

So we need to relearn the skill of fixing our eyes on Things Unseen.

Fixing. The word in English has a playful ambiguity. It means to mend: to *fix* a leaky faucet. It means to fasten: to *fix* a bracket to a shelf. It means to rig, to tamper with, to prearrange: to *fix* the game. In the Greek, the verb *skopē*—"to fix"—doesn't carry this diversity of meanings. It simply connotes an intensity of gaze—a determined, attentive searching out. But the range of meanings in our own language is a happy accident, or a fugitive providence. When we fix our hearts and minds on things above, we practice all three things at once: We mend—we *fix*—our wayward attention, our inbred distractedness, our myopia; we fasten—we *fix*—that attention to unseen realities; and we rig—we *fix*—things so that, more and more, we glimpse heaven in places and situations where before we saw only shadows and surfaces.

Heaven is meant to be our *fixation*—our Big Fix. It's to be our deep secret, like being in love, where just the thought of it carries us through menial chores or imparts to us courage in the face of danger. We fix on it, and it fixes us.

This book is an attempt to help us in that *fixation:* to uncover eternity in our hearts, to recover the hope of forever, and to discover what makes us so heavenly-minded that we're of much earthly good.

May you ever after be heaven-bent, your eyes fixed on Things Unseen, and convinced of this: Even though I die, yet shall I live.

Shalom,

Mark Buchanan

January 2002

PART I

HEAVEN-HAUNTED: MISSING THINGS UNSEEN

ONE

ETERNITY IN OUR HEARTS

I have a memory that lives in me now like the ache of an old wound, like shrapnel closed up in my flesh. It is of my mother and father laughing. Laughter spills from them, candy from a burst piñata, and my brother and I scramble to be part of it, to get a handful, a mouthful, a life full.

We are on holiday. My father, whose work to him was often a heaviness and a dreariness, is light from two weeks of rest and play and silence. His chronic irritability, his swift, jerky snapping at things, is gone. He often looked as if he was constantly fighting invisible restraints—a failed Houdini who, no matter how much he thrust and twisted to loose the ropes and chains, couldn't slip free. But his usual motions of rigid haste have slowed and smoothed, and the things that three weeks ago would have made him explode in anger or withdraw in sullenness now just make him shrug or chuckle. My mother has relaxed into my father's softening mood. She has almost collapsed into it, thankful, weary, only now realizing how close she herself was to breaking.

We're in a cabin beside the sea, and it's morning. The sun comes up hot, sweet. It shimmers bright on the skin of things. Light pours into the room; even the shadows brim with it. The small cabin fills up with the smells of coffee and maple bacon and buttered toast. You can sleep in if you want, but no one wants to. My father is busy in the kitchen, cooking, singing. My mother is on the deck of the cabin, reading. She comes in.

Something goes wrong. I don't remember what. The toast burns, or the coffee spills, or something breaks. In the huge shuddering silence that follows, I brace myself for anger, shouting, accusation.

But my parents laugh. It's a sound so pure that it could be grief. Wind chimes and birdsong and jingling coins and splashing brooks. Ancient holy secrets revealed, fresh news of triumph borne in on the wind. Fire and water and earth and air.

Laughter.

In that laughter, in the clean deep wide-openness of it, all things are possible. All things are forgotten, or remembered, accepted, forgiven, relinquished. That laughter is a sign as consoling as a fig branch in a dove's beak, a promise as dazzling as a rainbow arched over a world washed fresh. It is a pledge that the earth will not be destroyed as before.

I remember that.

It haunts me now.

My father is dead. He was talking on the phone one day—to the cardiologist, ironically—and his heart seized up. He pressed his hand hard to his chest, and staggered to where my mother sat in the other room. He sat down, gasping like a caught fish, and she stood up and phoned the ambulance. But the damage was too massive. He died shortly after, in the hospital.

I was on an island, on the first day of three weeks of holidays. My wife and I had just put the children to bed and unpacked the groceries. We were sitting down, making tea. A knock on the door. I answered. A man I didn't know was standing there holding a piece of paper.

"Are you Mark?"

"Yes."

"You're to phone your brother."

The man gave me the paper and walked off, a shadow among falling shadows. My brother's phone number was on the paper. He was scheduled to come with his family to visit us the next day. Things come up all the time—cars break down, unexpected guests arrive, extra work waylays us, interruptions delay us—so this message at nightfall should not have startled me, should not have filled me with any particular foreboding. But it did. Somehow I knew.

I walked down to the government wharf to the pay phone. I dialed the number. My brother answered, first ring, his voice thin and flat like the edge of hammered metal.

"Dad's dead. He had a heart attack. I guess there was nothing they could do."

I don't remember much else. I remember putting the phone down gently, as I might have a porcelain figurine, and then waiting in the quietness of the phone booth, not wanting to turn around. Not knowing what to do. Then walking up the hill to the cottage and my wife coming down, somehow knowing too.

"My dad died," I said. We held each other and cried.

My mother lives with her cats now. Often she talks to them as if they were people, very young people or very old people, people she feels the need to scold and dote on all at once. Her cats are aging, arthritic, mangy, glaucomatous. They hiss at children and hobble as they walk. My mother watches documentaries on television, and her cats curl around her, shedding fistfuls of hair.

And me, living far away—I have more things to keep up with than I can keep up with, and some nights I don't sleep well: Some gnawing and tugging inside keeps me half-awake half the night. I shed most of my hair when I was still young. My teeth are crooked; I never got that fixed, and now it's too late. The phone rings morning till night with grating and merciless urgency, and very seldom is it someone just wanting to say "I love you" (my mother still does that, though). Now I have e-mail, too, and each morning a new landslide of messages, much of it dirt and stone, tumbles in, threatening to engulf me. At any given time—I learned this several years ago now—someone somewhere is angry at or disappointed with me.

That bright summer when, in the fullness of their youth and mine, my parents laughed, is an archetypal myth to me now. It is a memory that became a dream that became a haunting. Thinking on it, I am both happy and sad. At once. It's almost too painful to remember and certainly too beautiful to forget. It speaks more things to me than I can know or explain.

It is eternity in my heart. It is a taste, however elusive, of some Other Thing, some Unseen Thing. It is a reminder that the world is not enough, and that every bone and cell in me knows that. It is a desire for something that earth can make me thirst for, but never quench.

There is a moment like that in Israel's history. The people have returned, straggle-wise, from exile and have begun to rebuild the destroyed temple. That destruction, at the hands of Nebuchadnezzar's Babylonian warriors in 586 B.C., represents the nation's biggest tragedy: the loss of the center. It represents either the defeat of God, or God's abandonment of His people. Either prospect is a huge desolation, a grief bigger than time itself. It is a wound that never quite heals: shrapnel closed up in the flesh.

But the people are back, the rebuilding has begun, and the moment has come when the long-cherished hope first touches reality: The foundation is laid. Finished. There it is, as real as earth and fire. You can dance on it, if you want, or kiss it. It is a stone you could stumble over.

And that calls for a party. If there is one thing the Hebrew people knew how to do right, it was party.

When the builders laid the foundation of the temple of the
LORD, the priests in their vestments and with trumpets, and
the Levites (the sons of Asaph) with cymbals, took their places
to praise the LORD, as prescribed by David king of Israel. With
praise and thanksgiving they sang to the LORD: "He is good;
his love to Israel endures forever." And all the people gave a
great shout of praise to the LORD, because the foundation of
the house of the LORD was laid. (Ezra 3:10–11)

But the celebration is haunted. Something is amiss; literally, something is missing.

But many of the older priests and Levites and family heads,
who had seen the former temple, wept aloud when they saw
the foundation of this temple being laid, while many others
shouted for joy. No one could distinguish the sound of the
shouts of joy from the sound of weeping, because the people
made so much noise. And the sound was heard far away. (Ezra
3:12–13)

The archetype is this: All that weeping and laughing, heard a long
way off, one indistinguishable from the other, is what we all feel at all
our homecomings, all our foundation-layings. They are moments of
great joy, and yet also sadness. Even the best foundations—even the
first ones, the pristine ones—fall short of what we *remember*.

We know, and can't escape the knowing, that even when we

come home, we are still in exile and that all the foundations we lay, no matter how glorious and solid, are at best only shadows of what we hoped for.

> By faith he made his home in the promised land *like a stranger in a foreign country; he lived in tents,* as did Isaac and Jacob, who were heirs with him of the same promise. For he was looking forward to the city with foundations, whose architect and builder is God. (Hebrews 11:9–10, emphasis added)

Even in a land flowing with milk and honey, we live estranged, we dwell in tents. It simply doesn't matter how good earth gets or how much we experience our settlement here as promised land. No foundation we lay can take away our sense that we're not home yet. The apostle Paul puts it this way: "Now we know that if the earthly tent we live in is destroyed, we have a building from God, an eternal house in heaven, not built by human hands. Meanwhile we groan, longing to be clothed with our heavenly dwelling" (2 Corinthians 5:1–2).

This is eternity in our hearts. This is being haunted with and wooed by Things Unseen.

Things Unseen. God calls us to live among them, to set our sights on them, to treasure them against all sorrow, loss, doubt, disappointment.

But isn't that escapism?

No. It's the truest realism.

J. R. R. Tolkien was often accused of writing escapist literature, of conjuring up a world that indulged the human longing to slip the boredom and burden of living our nine-to-five, hand-to-mouth, this-and-that lives. His answer was that there are two kinds of escape.

The first is the escape of one who is running away from life, who can't endure its disappointments and responsibilities. It's the painter Paul Gauguin, who abandoned his wife and children to try to capture some earthly paradise in Tahiti, or Jean Jacques Rousseau, who kept dumping his illegitimate children in orphanages so he could pursue his ambitions to write about the perfection of child-rearing. This form of escape is hypocritical and pathetic.

But there is a second kind of escape. It is the escape of the prisoner of war, who seeks to break out of the grim, muddy compound, with its scowling guards, its snarling dogs, its shockingly dreadful threats and numbingly dull routines, its guns and fleas and gruel. All he wants—and it is a huge want, able to carry him when nothing else can—is to go home. This form of escape keeps us human.

Tolkien said that he was writing about the second kind of escapism, not the first.[1]

If heavenly-mindedness is a form of escapism, it is of the second kind: a remembrance and an expectancy—a groaning for home. A longing that sustains us no matter how dark it gets.

Heavenly-mindedness is sanity. It is the best regimen for keeping our hearts whole, our minds clear. It allows us to enjoy earth's pleasures without debauchery. It allows us to endure life's agonies without despair. It allows us to see things from the widest possible perspective and in the truest possible proportions. If anything can give us a true scale of values—one that enables us to sort out the disposable from the precious, the trinkets from the treasures, the surface from the substance—heavenly-mindedness can.

The church has lost this, and our losing it has happened with little dismay and hardly any remark. We live, in A. J. Conyers's phrase, beneath the "eclipse of heaven."[2] When we feel mildly provoked to justify this, we do so with the shopworn slogan: You don't want to become so heavenly-minded that you're of no earthly good.

You'd sooner find an atheist in a foxhole or a Green Peace activist on a foxhunt than find a Christian, living or dead, fitting that description. Biblically and historically, the exact opposite is true: Those who have cultivated a genuine heavenly-mindedness—who have named and nurtured the human longing for Elsewhere and Otherwise—have been people who have worked and prayed the most passionately, courageously, tirelessly, and unswervingly for the kingdom to come on earth as it is in heaven.

C. S. Lewis notes:

If you read history, you will find that the Christians who did the most for the present world were just those who thought most of the next. The apostles themselves, who set on foot the conversion of the Roman Empire, the great men who built up the Middle Ages, the English evangelicals who abolished the slave trade, all left their mark on earth, precisely because their minds were occupied with heaven. It is since Christians have largely ceased to think of the other world that they have become so ineffective in this.[3]

Indeed.

Only those who fill their hearts and minds with heaven can want or even recognize its earthly counterpart. Only they can seek after it in a way that indulges neither utopian dreams nor despotic solutions. To be of real earthly good requires a certain fearlessness: a freedom from the fear of death, from the loss of property or status or title or comfort, from the threat of tyrants, the power of armies, the day of trouble.

People fixated on earth generally do not have this deep taproot of courage and conviction. Seldom do they stand down Pharaohs, Caesars, Stalins, with nothing but a stick in their hand or a cross on their back. Nor do they generally look after widows and orphans in distress or care for the dying or feed the hungry. This is left for the heavenly-minded to do—for the Stephens, whose serving meals to widows and confronting the powers of the age were all of a piece, and who, at the very edge of his brutal execution, "looked up to heaven and saw the glory of God" (Acts 7:55).

Like the tug and heft of a huge unseen planet hovering near, the hope of heaven is meant to exert a gravitational pull that gives our lives stability, substance, weight. Ironically, it alone has the power to give us in a sustained way the moral and spiritual ballast needed to keep our feet on the earth—to make us of much earthly good. It is a rumor of home in a place of exile, inspiring us to keep up the good work.

It is Unseen Things that render the things we do see—both the beauty and the ugliness, the grandeur and the barrenness, never enough, and yet never too much.

Two

SPEAKING IN TONGUES

Some mornings, it's all I can do to get up.

My bones are deadlocked and wayward both, my muscles cramped yet ropy. Daylight falls at sharp angles into the room, like glass shards scattered. The light is gray or gold, depending on the weather, but neither holds any charm, extends any invitation. I lie there, slumped and crumpled. I groan.

At forty-one, I'm in fairly good shape. I ride my bike more than I drive. I read novels, history, theology, poetry. I listen to an eclectic selection of music, from Dire Straits to Diana Krall, from Hill Songs to Brahms. I have meaningful and interesting work to do: preaching, teaching, counseling, writing, leading. I get to travel a fair amount, when it's convenient for me and usually at someone else's expense. I garden, and I have never stopped being amazed at the way the hard earth yields and softens at the turn of a spade and how tiny seeds buried there resurrect as flowers or food.

I have a beautiful family: a wife who is healthy, funny, pretty—and a good cook—and three children who are strong, smart, and growing like they ought to. I have fine neighbors, who swap eggs or sugar or video head cleaners with us as needed, who take in our mail when we're away, who wave to us when we drive past, even if we're just going to the corner store for milk. I have good friends and spend time with them just enjoying companionship, laughter, food.

My life is good—as good as it gets.

Yet I spend a lot of time groaning, and not just in the morning.

Is this just another pathetic story of selfishness, of a shallow but ever-empty man who takes and takes and yet never truly receives? Who is bloated but never full? Who devours but doesn't savor, hoards but never treasures, for whom all the riches and pleasures of earth would not suffice?

Maybe.

Or maybe it's this: Some groaning is holy speech, another kind of speaking in tongues.

For I can also testify that I am a deeply thankful man, often wonder-struck, and that most days I have a genuine sense of God's nearness, His solace and rebuke, His strong hand upon me. Over and over I have tasted and seen that the Lord is good—good when the grain silos or fishnets are full, good when the field yields no crop and the olive tree does not blossom. Good all the time. I have come to the same conclusion the writer of Ecclesiastes did:

I know that there is nothing better for men than to be happy and do good while they live. That everyone may eat and drink, and find satisfaction in all his toil—this is the gift of God.

Go, eat your food with gladness, and drink your wine with a joyful heart, for it is now that God favors what you do.

Enjoy life with your wife, whom you love…. Whatever your hand finds to do, do it with all your might.

Now all has been heard; here is the conclusion of the matter: Fear God and keep his commandments, for this is the whole duty of man. (Ecclesiastes 3:12–13; 9:7, 9–10; 12:13)

I have embraced the insight to which the apostle Paul attained:

I know what it is to be in need, and I know what it is to have plenty. I have learned the secret of being content in any and every situation, whether well fed or hungry, whether living in plenty or in want. I can do everything through him who gives me strength. (Philippians 4:12–13)

All this is true. And still, I groan.

Groaning is homesickness.

"When God wants to carry a point with his children," Emerson said, "He plants his argument into the instincts." Our deepest instinct is heaven. Heaven is the ache in our bones, the splinter in our heart. Like the whisper of faraway waves we hear crashing in the whorls of a conch shell, the music of heaven echoes, faint, elusive, haunting, beneath and within our daily routines.

There you are, standing at a window watching oak leaves flutter down from dark boughs, and without warning your whole body fills with a longing for something you can't name, something you've lost but never had, that you're nostalgic for yet don't remember. You sense a joy so huge it breaks you, a sorrow so deep it cleanses.

Or in line at a store one day, you turn and look at a child who doesn't notice you. The skin on her face curves down flushed and smooth along her cheekbones and creases into delicate folds at her eyes. There is a wild hope in those eyes, and her beauty pierces you in a way you don't understand.

Or you listen to Ralph Vaughan Williams's *The Lark Ascending,* and somehow it is both laughter and mourning, spring and winter, homecoming and exile. It makes you feel supple and playful and young and yet old, with brittle bones and trembling hands. And you wonder: *How can this be?*

This is how: You want to go home. The instinct for heaven is just that: homesickness, ancient as night, urgent as daybreak. All your longings—for the place you grew up, for the taste of raspberry tarts that your mother once pulled hot from the oven, for that bend in the river where your father took you fishing as a child, where the water was dark and swirling and the caddis flies hovered in the deep shade—all these longings are a homesickness, a wanting in full what all these things only hint at, only prick you with. These are the things seen that conjure in our emotions the Things Unseen. "He has set eternity in the hearts of men," the writer of Ecclesiastes said; "yet they cannot fathom what God has done from beginning to end" (3:11).

—〜—

Groaning is the lexicon and grammar of our *dis*-location, our sense of being in the wrong place. It is our mother tongue, the speech we fall back on when we can't recall the words to speak in earth language, that foreign tongue we're trying to learn to speak fluently but keep garbling.

Ursula was a long-standing member of my first church. She was a widow in her eighties. She was originally from Germany, and though she had lived in Canada for more than fifty years, she had never lost the thickness in her accent, the stiffness in her phrasing. A gangly, makeshift grammar framed her speech.

As Ursula grew older and her memory grew threadbare, her English—more than fifty years in the making—washed out of her. Fifty years of words and phrases, carefully accumulated, sorted, and filed, began to vanish. I would visit her, and she would try to communicate the simplest thoughts—that the doctor had changed her prescription for high blood pressure, or that her neighbor cut his lawn too early in the morning and disturbed her prayers, or that her ankles were terribly swollen and kept her from sleeping at night—but she couldn't find the words in English to say these things.

She would mutter, stammer, shake her head, pound the table, and then let out a slew of German words so forceful that it was like cursing. I would sit there bewildered. She would glower, her face cast in stony fierceness, a Teutonic warrior churlish with gout, ready to slay me for my weakness and stupidity. "Ursula," I'd say, "I'm sorry. I don't understand." And she would fling, like fistfuls of sharp rocks, more German words at me.

That's what I mean. Groaning is our default language, our mother tongue. It is the language we remember when we forget all others—the language of an ancient memory we carry like a dream and a sorrow.

Paul tells us that the Spirit takes our groaning and sings it in a deeper key. "The Spirit helps us in our weakness," he says. "The Spirit himself intercedes for us with groans that words cannot express" (Romans 8:26). *With groans that words cannot express.* Angelspeak, this. By some lexical alchemy, the Spirit Himself takes our earth-speech, in all its bluntness and slipperiness, its stiffness and clumsiness, and translates it into heaven-speech. The Spirit testifies by groaning—by giving voice to our yearning for God and giving testimony to God's yearning for us. By uttering that which words cannot express: our wordless longing for Things Unseen.

Back in the late eighties, my brother, Adam, and his wife, Leslie, were living in Bangkok, Thailand. My wife, Cheryl, and I visited them. That was before any of us had children. We went to the typical tourist attractions: the gaudy spectacle of the Grand Palace, the muddy labyrinth of Bangkok's canals—its *klongs*—and the pearly beaches of Phuket.

Adam worked for a relief and development organization, and so he was able to take us to some of the nontourist sites as well: a refugee camp at the edge of the border, where Khmer Rouge, their bodies darkly etched with ritual tattoos and pocked and ridged with scars, looked at us with unbreakable hardness; a slum, where for fun children kicked to death a chicken with a rope tied around its neck, its feathers flying like a burst pillow, its scrawny body jerking wildly beneath the blows.

And he took us to an orphanage on the outskirts of Bangkok. We drove out of the city, where the land opened up into silty flats and, in the distance, mountains rose dark against a storm-churned sky. After a while, we turned off the highway and continued on down a dirt road raised up between stretches of rice paddies, gleaming wet and bristling with rice grass. Farther down, at the edge of one of the rice fields, stood a series of plain buildings, with a hand-painted sign at the entrance. This was the orphanage. The worker who met us at the front entrance told us to feel free to visit where we wished. We walked in, not sure where to begin.

We needn't have worried: The children came to us, ran to us, clung to us. They were starved for touch and voice. They could not get close enough to us. We each carried around several children, while others hung onto our legs and arms. They pressed their faces, dusted with talc to cool their skin in the sweltering heat, into our skin and clothes, smelling our living bodies, some of them gathering a shirt-sleeve or collar into their mouth and sucking it. They caressed our faces, plucked gently at the hair on our arms. They didn't understand a single word we spoke, and yet they did—they understood the tenderness, the goodwill.

Leaving that orphanage was one of the hardest things I've ever done. We literally had to peel the children off of us—to pry loose their tiny clutching hands, unwrap their thin, entwining legs—and push them off, while the workers pulled them away and held them back. Many of the children wept and looked at us stricken, betrayed.

Then we drove away. In the car we were dead silent for a long time. We listened to the hum, hugely amplified in the car's hot interior, of the tires on the rough pavement. We listened to the blood sluicing through our veins and the wind needling through the door cracks. We watched bugs accumulate, in black flecks and bright spatters, on the windshield. When we finally began to talk, none of us mentioned the orphanage. None of us were able to, not for a long season.

Later, that experience spoke many things to me. But this is the one I wish to pass on: The longing in us for the Parent is so deep, so desperate, that deprived of Him, any stranger will do.

These children haunt me. Many years later, I still see their dark eyes, bright at our appearing, emptied and extinguished at our departing. I see their chalky skin, as though they'd pressed their faces, sweat-dampened, into a bag of white flour. I can feel the tight brace of their hands on my arm, the tugging of their arms around my neck, the winching coil of their legs around my waist.

For one hour, I was the father they never knew. For one glorious, tragic hour, I entered their life, they entered mine, and the world was as it ought to be. For one hour, I felt, I think, what God feels.

—ɯ—

But that wasn't all. That morning in the orphanage, we visited another building, off behind the main buildings. We entered a room darkened with shades. There were several cribs crowded together, and in each was a child. The children were small, frail, in diapers, but most of them weren't infants. Some of them were eight or nine years old. These children did not respond to us. No smiles. No laughter. No embrace. No speech. No eye contact. They lay still, curled up tight, or sat rocking in their cribs, staring blank-eyed. We spoke to them, stroked their arms and backs, picked them up. But there was an inertness in their flesh, like touching dead wood. It was as though we weren't there. It was as though *they* weren't there.

Some of the children were silent.

But most of them groaned.

They had been alone so long—untouched, unnoticed, unloved—that they had closed up inside themselves. All that was left, or all that seeped out, was the groaning.

Paul says that the whole creation groans, waiting for the sons of God—for you and me—to be *revealed*, to come into the fullness of our inheritance and identity, to be filled to full with God's Spirit.

The Spirit himself testifies with our spirit that we are God's children. The creation waits in eager expectation for the sons of God to be revealed.

We know that the whole creation has been groaning as in

the pains of childbirth right up to the present time. Not only so, but we ourselves, who have the firstfruits of the Spirit, groan inwardly as we wait eagerly for our adoption as sons, the redemption of our bodies. (Romans 8:16, 19, 22–23)

What is this groaning except, at root, a longing for heaven? A longing that no father on earth, no matter how attentive and affectionate, can quite satisfy? A longing for all that's hidden and broken and scattered now to be gathered and mended and *revealed:* for the kingdom to come on earth as it is in heaven? A longing for the Father to make His sons what His sons are not yet?

We hear the groaning in all things. In orphans. In refugees. In housewives, in businessmen, from history professors, from folk musicians. In the sated. In the famished. In the sleek, the sick, the wounded, the pampered. In victims and victors. We hear it in haiku poetry, in country-and-western laments, in street marches, in hunger strikes. We hear it in the rocks beneath the earth's crust as they tremble and slip, in the wood joists of our houses at night as they shiver and pull, in the bones of our bodies as they shudder and twist. We hear it in our guts. We hear it in our heads. We hear it in our hearts.

It is a whisper.

It is a thunder.

We hear it, and if you do not, then like unto a stone is your deafness.

Now we know that if the earthly tent we live in is destroyed, we have a building from God, an eternal house in heaven, not built by human hands. Meanwhile we groan, longing to be clothed with our heavenly dwelling.

Now it is God who has made us for this very purpose and has given us the Spirit as a deposit, guaranteeing what is to come. (2 Corinthians 5:1–2, 5, emphasis added)

Now it is God who has made us for this very purpose.

I don't speak in tongues. But I have come to accept groaning as holy speech, the fire in my bones rising up, taking voice. It's the ache in creation echoed in me, answered by the Spirit. I don't stoke that fire. But I don't quench it, either, for this is the Spirit's testimony, His guarantee of what is to come. This is my eager expectation: that one day, the Father will come through the door, adoption papers in hand. And He won't leave without me.

Until then, homesick, I groan.

THREE

THE WORLD
IS NOT ENOUGH

Peter was dying. For many years, Peter, like his biblical namesake, had made his living pulling fish from the sea. He was a good man, honest, hardworking, loyal. He was a local hero of sorts, a doer of kind deeds, a puller of benign pranks—Good Samaritan and practical joker all in one.

Peter was my wife's uncle. He never attended church, but honestly, I wish more of those who did possessed half his kindness or a quarter his generosity. He sat before me now, wrapped in blankets, brittle and shivering. His sturdy frame had become rickety. His mind skittered between weary distraction and startling lucidity. His laughter was still there—a good earthy chortle—but the robustness had all spilled out of it.

We desperately wanted him to live. He himself, and those of us who loved him, remained resolutely focused on the hope of that. He was going to try a new treatment, and maybe it would work. Today was a better day than yesterday; he had more strength, went for a walk, and so maybe the worst was behind him. He'd been a few days into a new special diet, and this might do the trick.

But none of it did. Peter died a week later. I had the honor of leading his memorial service. I met with Peter's wife, Patricia, and two of his four children, Jean and Patty, to discuss the service. They were expecting eighty, maybe a hundred people. Several friends and family members wanted to say words of reminiscence and tribute. I asked if I could say something also, a brief meditation from the Bible, and they agreed that this would be good. They teasingly referred to my part as "Mark's religious gobbledygook."

Eighty people didn't come to the memorial service. One hundred didn't. Over five hundred people came. Suddenly, everyone was scrambling to accommodate the crowd. I was master of ceremonies, there to introduce, quickly and quietly, the various eulogizers and tribute-payers. This list, too, had grown. There were friends who knew him when he was young; friends who met him late in life. Golf buddies, fishing pals, neighbors. Work colleagues. Brothers-in-law. Sons and daughters, grandsons and granddaughters, nieces and nephews. A group of a dozen or so ladies who sang for him. His good wife, Pat. Each told their funny or moving stories, sang folk songs and show tunes, repeated Peter's favorite wisecracks and adages, recalled his kind deeds and mischievous pranks.

Then it was my turn. The service had stretched to nearly two hours, and I sensed everyone was tired and I had best keep it very brief. I wrestled with what to say. I had prepared notes, but they now seemed beside the point: religious gobbledygook indeed. For two hours, Peter had lived in our remembrances, and we were all aching with missing him. I stood up. In front of the podium were three large tables laid with mementos of Peter's life: several photo albums showing him from babyhood through his teen years and marriage and early fatherhood, right up to his last months, his last days. There was a bottle of Scotch, chain saw pants and old leather gloves and logger's tools, golf paraphernalia and fishing tackle, rifles and nautical instruments, a jar of his favorite marmalade, a box of his favorite biscuits.

If anything, it all evoked Peter too strongly. It made his absence worse.

"So," I said, "is this Peter's life? Is this what a life is, what a life distills to—these stories, these fond and funny memories, these keepsakes and scrapbooks, these collections and recollections?

"I don't care what religion you belong to or would never belong to, what beliefs you profess or scorn. I would bet a sweet purse that every one of you in this room has an instinct, and that the instinct is sharp as a razor right now.

"The instinct is that the world is not enough. The instinct is that this world isn't big enough, long enough, deep enough to contain or explain even one single life in it. The instinct is that death, no matter how natural its causes, is always unnatural, a brusque intruder, a gloating enemy, and that death shouldn't be allowed to have the last word. The instinct is that we weren't made for this world only. We were made for eternity. The world is not enough."

Did you think it was?

In 1988, doctors discovered a malignant tumor in the throwing arm of Dave Dravecky, star pitcher for the San Francisco Giants. They removed the tumor, and Dravecky returned to the game. Thankful, joyful, he wrote a book about it, *Comeback*. But in 1991, he had to have his pitching arm amputated. Out of that experience he wrote another book, *When You Can't Come Back*. He writes:

> I miss doing things with my own two hands, and—of course—I really miss baseball. There is a scene in the movie *Field of Dreams* where Shoeless Joe Jackson said, "Getting thrown out of baseball was like having part of me amputated. I'd wake up at night with the smell of the ballpark in my nose, the cool of the grass on my feet. Man, did I love this game. I'd have played for food money.... I'd have played for nuthin'."
>
> The scene had a powerful effect on me. I missed those feelings too. The feel of stitched seams as you cradle a new ball in your hand. The smell of seasoned leather as you bring the glove to your face. The sound of a bat cracking out a base hit. I'd have played for food money. I'd have played for nuthin'.[4]

The seventeenth-century philosopher, mathematician, and theologian Blaise Pascal gave a reason for this missing. Do you miss, he asked, something you've never had? Do you grieve the absence of a third leg, or the loss of a second pair of eyes? No. We ache only when something we once knew, held, tasted, goes missing. We sorrow over the eyes or legs or arms we once had and then lost, not over those we never had. So why is it that our heart feels this harrowing absence, this desolate sense of loss? What are we missing?

Marshall Shelley, an editor for *Leadership* magazine, had a child that lived only two minutes. Toby. Toby entered the world at 8:20 P.M. on November 22, 1991, and departed the world at 8:22. "My wife Susan and I," Marshall writes, "never got to see him take his first steps. We barely got to see him take his first breath. I don't know if he would have enjoyed softball or software, dinosaurs or dragonflies. We never got to wrestle, race, or read.... What would have made him laugh? Made him scared? Made him angry?"

Toby was born with a rare and severe genetic disorder. Three months after he was born and died, Marshall and Susan Shelley's two-year-old daughter, Mandy, died. In the wake of these two devastating losses, the Shelleys wrestled with God. *Why, God? Why did You do that? What was all that about?* "Why," Marshall asks, "did God create a child to live two minutes?" He answers:

He didn't. [And] He didn't create Mandy to live two years. He did not create me to live 40 years (or whatever number he may choose to extend my days in this world).

God created Toby for eternity. He created each of us for eternity, where we may be surprised to find our true calling, which always seemed just out of reach here on earth.[5]

Isn't that how you feel much of the time? That what you want the most—and most of the time you're not even sure what that is—seems always out of reach? That your most robust laughter rings with the echo of your weeping? That your most joyous homecomings are haunted at the edges by unnameable sorrows? That your victories and breakthroughs are mixed with complaint and doubt? That something's always missing?

We were not created for earth alone. We were created for eternity.

And all our deepest senses confirm it. Our *missing* something we can never find confirms it. Last year I saw the accomplishment of a lifelong dream: I held in my hand my first published book. Twenty years of dreaming. Eight years of writing. All the labyrinth of contracts and editing and marketing and distributing finished. All the prayers and hopes and efforts converging in one glorious moment.

And it wasn't enough. It didn't forever satisfy me. It didn't take away all my hunger, all my fears. It didn't answer all my longings or quell all my insecurities. It didn't fulfill me.

"Well, aren't you a spoiled brat," you might say.

But imagine something for a moment. Imagine that such accomplishments are all there is. Imagine that our tragedies do have the last word. Imagine that our triumphs are the highest heights we'll ever attain. Imagine that this is as good as it gets.

Is it enough?

The writer of Ecclesiastes—I've already hinted at this—may be our best guide here. He undertook a hugely ambitious life experiment and, like one of those half-mad, half-noble, utterly obsessed scientists that movies love to caricature, he made himself the guinea pig, the lab rat, the one who tests on himself the serum that might transform him, angel-like, but will just as likely deform him, monster-like. *What would be enough?* he wonders. *Is there something, anything, many things that would fill this hollow place in me? Is there some satisfaction so potent that it could satisfy my need to be satisfied?*

Away he went. He threw himself headlong into every manner of thing he could contrive, everything his vast wealth could procure, his sweeping power secure, his fecund imagination conjure. "I denied myself nothing my eyes desired; I refused my heart no pleasure" (Ecclesiastes 2:10). The noble. The debased. The intellectual. The sensual. The cultural. The carnal. He built things, wrote things, amassed things, squandered things. He created and he destroyed. He drank himself silly. He bedded a thousand women and more. He wielded despotic power. He enslaved himself to the tyranny of madness. He pierced the heights and plumbed the depths, tested the soul's outer bounds and inner reaches. Nothing in all creation separated him from doing whatever he wanted, taking whatever he sought.

And it was empty, all of it. He found, indeed, that each new experience left him feeling a little more blasé, desperate, jaded, broken. Nothing was enough. Everything wasn't enough. All was vanity, chasing wind, wasting time. Meaningless.

Weary and chastened, he wrote his book, Ecclesiastes: a chronicle of folly, a diary of all the ways we can lose our life by trying to save it.

There is wisdom here, too, wisdom gleaned at the far edge of heartache and sin, salvaged from the ruins of wasted time. The wisdom distills, mostly, to an earthy common sense, a proverbial shrewdness: love well, go slow, work hard, say thanks, make do; let what you have be enough. It's a fine conclusion. We might have expected him to counsel some world-denying, flesh-defying asceticism, a regimen of rigorous self-mortification: Live in a cave; scourge your body; purge your insides; eat locusts. But he doesn't. He advises simple contentment, modest pleasure, honest work, evenhanded moderation.

But there is also a glimpse toward something else. The Old Testament gives only a few hints about life beyond the grave. The doctrine of heaven in the Old Covenant is only seed-like, a tiny thing, elusive and dormant. It is easily missed. But the writer of Ecclesiastes saw it. Even in the midst of his cynicism and exhaustion—or perhaps because of that—he saw it: "I have seen the burden God has laid on men. He has made everything beautiful in its time. He has also set eternity in the hearts of men; yet they cannot fathom what God has done from beginning to end" (Ecclesiastes 3:10–11).

The world, beautiful as it is, is not enough. The beauty itself doesn't satisfy. It promises satisfaction that, mirage-like, it can't provide. Yet the beauty is a mimetic clue, both echo and foretaste, of Things Unseen, an enigmatic hint of Elsewhere which we puzzle over but rarely decipher. He has set eternity in the hearts of men; yet they cannot fathom what God has done. He is everywhere baiting us, prodding, luring us. He is playing hide-and-seek with heaven and earth, strewing clues all around, brushing the commonplace with the scent of Things Unseen.

Making us always wish for more, and always coming up short.

Richard John Neuhaus tells about Dr. Irvin D. Yalom, a Stanford professor and psychiatrist who regularly leads group therapy sessions. The people in the group—strangers to each other—are paired together at random and then given a simple assignment: to each ask the other, repeatedly, one question: "What do you want?" Dr. Yalom writes:

Could anything be simpler? One innocent question and its answer. And yet, time after time, I have seen this group exercise evoke unexpectedly powerful feelings. Often, within minutes, the room rocks with emotion. Men and women—and these are by no means desperate or needy, but successful, well-functioning, well-dressed people who glitter as they walk—are stirred to the depths. They call out to those who are forever lost—dead or absent parents, spouses, children, friends: "I want to see you again." "I want your love." "I want to know you are proud of me." "I want you to know I love you and how sorry I am I never told you." "I want you back—I am so lonely." "I want the childhood I never had." So much wanting. So much longing. And so much pain, so close to the surface, only minutes deep. Destiny pain. Existence pain. Pain that is always there, whirring continually just beneath the membrane of life.[6]

So much wanting. So much longing. And so much pain. Destiny pain.

What if the "so much wanting" is for something earth doesn't have? What if the world that is, even if you gain it all, is not enough, and will never be, and was never meant to be?

Then what?

FOUR

RICH AND WEARY

Homesickness—this perpetual experience of missing something—usually gets misdiagnosed and so wrongly treated. The writer of Ecclesiastes himself misunderstood his own ache, and he went off in the vain pursuit of something, anything, to fill him up. It's an old story, and a daily one. All our lives we take hold of the wrong thing, go to the wrong place, eat the wrong food. We drink too much, sleep too much, work too long, take too many vacations or too few—all in the faint hope that this will finally satisfy us and so silence the hunger within. We go from relationship to relationship, job to job, house to house, church to church, convinced that this one is the right one.

It's not.

And it won't ever be. Better to figure it out now: The world is booby-trapped. It's rigged for disappointment. On earth everything falls short of some hoped-for ideal. Everything good down here has a tragic brevity and a funny aftertaste to it. It all falls short and shortly falls apart. None of it possesses any ultimacy.

In response, we can become so cynical that we poison ourselves, so self-indulgent that we devour ourselves, so despairing that we collapse into ourselves. In fact, self-pity and self-indulgence, boredom and despair, envy and greed—such are only yearning gone sour. They are just the greasy residue that remains after yearning has gone unfulfilled too many times. A sadness like ash settles on our doings and our desires. We find trinkets to fiddle with, trivia to distract us. A once-burning zeal dwindles to a dry itch, and everything becomes a frantic attempt to get the passion back, or a plodding resignation to its death.

A few years ago I wrote an article about consumerist culture for *Christianity Today* called "Trapped in the Cult of the Thing." In it I examine how we continually live for the Next Thing—the next purchase, the next weekend, the next job, the next adventure. This becomes so obsessive that we lose the capacity to enjoy and to be thankful for *this* thing we have right now or *that* thing we got yesterday. Consumerism teaches us not to value things too much, but to value them too little. We forget how to treasure and to savor. The pressure of constant wanting dissipates all gratitude. The weight of restless craving plunders all enjoyment.[7]

I saw this close-up a few years ago, when my children first got to that age when the essence of Christmas becomes The Day of Getting. There were mounds of gifts beneath our tree, and our son led the way in that favorite childhood (and, more subtly, adult) game, How Many Are For Me? But the telling moment came Christmas morning when the gifts were handed out. The children ripped through them, shredding and scattering the wrappings like jungle plants before a well-wielded machete.

Each gift was beautiful: an intricately laced dress Grandma Christie had sewn, an exquisitely detailed model car Uncle Bob had found at a specialty store on Robson Street in Vancouver, a finely bound and gorgeously illustrated collection of children's classics Aunt Leslie had sent. The children looked at each gift briefly, their interest quickly fading, and then put it aside to move on to the Next Thing. When the ransacking was finished, my son, standing amid a tumultuous sea of boxes and bright crumpled paper and exotic trappings, asked plaintively, "Is this all there is?"

"Meaningless, meaningless! Everything is meaningless!" That was the cry of the writer of Ecclesiastes after he had opened all the gifts and not found the one thing needed. "Is this all there is?"

Here is the surprise: God made us this way. He made us to yearn—to always be hungry for something we can't get, to always be missing something we can't find, to always be disappointed with what we receive, to always have an insatiable emptiness that no thing can fill and an untamable restlessness that no discovery can still. Yearning itself is healthy—a kind of compass inside us, pointing to True North.

It's not the wanting that corrupts us. What corrupts us is the wanting that's misplaced, set on the wrong thing. If we don't understand that—if we don't understand that God has set eternity in our hearts to make us heavenly-minded, we skew or subvert the yearning and scatter it in a thousand wrong directions. We take a God-imparted hunger and send it out grubbing for meals. We twist our God-shaped passion for treasure hunting into a rodentlike filching and scavenging. We shunt true longing into mere moping, zestful seeking into a murmuring sullenness.

But the cure for our yearning and our restlessness is not to keep getting more. That only bloats us, never fills us. Nor is the cure some Buddhistic detachment, where we try to winnow out from ourselves all passions and desires. That only depletes us, never cleanses us. The cure is to yearn for the right thing, the Unseen Things.

Yearning in its pure form is our deepest instinct for heaven. The seventeenth-century poet George Herbert captured this idea well in his poem "The Pulley":

When God at first made man
Having a glass of blessings standing by,
"Let us," said he, "pour on him all we can:
Let the world's riches, which dispersèd lie,
Contract into a span."

So strength first made a way;
Then beauty flowed, then wisdom, honor, pleasure.
When almost all was out, God made a stay,
Perceiving that, alone of all his treasure,
Rest in the bottom lay.

"For if I should," said he,
"Bestow this jewel also on my creature,
He would adore my gifts instead of me,
And rest in Nature, not the God of Nature;
So both should losers be.

"Yet let him keep the rest,
But keep them with repining restlessness.
Let him be rich and weary, that at least,
If goodness lead him not, yet weariness
May toss him to my breast."[8]

Let him keep the rest, but keep them with repining restlessness. Let him be rich and weary.

Rich and weary both. This is our condition. All earth's things fall short of fullness and finality. God Himself, Herbert suggests, has done this—has withheld from us the ability to fully treasure earth's riches, to fully savor its beauties. We are metaphysically handicapped. This is not so much a design flaw as a *designed* flaw, a glitch wired into the system, a planned obsolescence.

And on top of all that, earth exists in ruined glory. The world is not as it ought to be. Earth, only a shadow of heaven, is also only a shadow of itself. Between just these two things—our metaphysical handicap, creation's bondage to decay—it is clear enough why our time here is "of few days and full of trouble" (Job 14:1). Life is inherently unfinished. It is fissured with breaks, ridden with struggle, riddled with loss.

Yet we carry this secret desire, this fugitive hope, this implacable hunger for Unseen Things. God has created us with the knowledge of Elsewhere and Otherwise—of a place, in Herbert's words (which are simply St. Augustine's, which are simply those of the writer of Hebrews), of Rest, where all longings are not muted and not disappointed, but infinitely and eternally satisfied.

C. S. Lewis writes:

Creatures are not born with desires unless satisfaction for those desires exists. A baby feels hunger: well, there is such a thing as food. A duckling wants to swim: well, there is such a thing as water. Men feel sexual desire: well, there is such a thing as sex. If I find in myself a desire which no experience in this world can satisfy, the most probable explanation is that I was made for another world. If none of my earthly pleasures satisfy it, that does not mean the universe is a fraud…earthly pleasures were never meant to satisfy it, but only to arouse it, to suggest the real thing.[9]

This shaking, unslaked desire in me is a divining rod for streams of Living Water. This unfilled, seemingly unfillable hunger that gnaws me and drives me is an appetite for ambrosia, the food of God. He did it: He put in me, in you, a homing device for heaven. We just won't *settle* for anything less.

—∞—

Lewis called earth "the Shadowlands." There is genius in that. Earth is the land where even the most exquisite beauty or sheerest joy has strands of dark lying across it, a hint and taint of eclipse. Our most robust joy is haunted with sorrow.

I have stood atop a peak in central British Columbia, looking down at granite and pine, lichen and moraine, the earth stretching away in dizzying panoramic wildness. The wind gripped my body like an angel wrestling me and stung my skin with a cleanness like first love, and I felt both huge and small, conquered and conquering, afraid and undaunted. And yet, even immersed in such exhilaration, I felt the flattening, hollowing power of boredom.

I have been at reunions with people I love and longed to see, and in the midst of a gale of laughter sweeping through the room, I felt a shiver of loneliness twine down my bones.

I have swum among the shoals of water-sculpted rock and schools of bright, darting fish, my body ethereally light in the warm tropical surge of current, and all the while a part of me wished I were somewhere else.

Why? Why is it that even while cavorting in a paradise of earthly delights, we sometimes can't conceal a yawn of apathy, a pang of disappointment, a nagging sense that something's missing?

We're rich and weary both, longing for Things Unseen. We're heaven-bent, all crooked until the light of forever straightens us up.

—m—

But that's not all. On earth, we not only miss heaven; we glimpse it too. We glimpse it, of course, in laughter and beauty and rest—in children playing and ducks flying in V-formation and a grandmother knitting a baby blanket.

But even in the darkest places, among bone shards and blood-stains, there are glints of light, drafts of warmth. My brother, a photo-journalist, has traveled to some of the world's worst killing fields—Vietnam, Cambodia, Burma, Bosnia, Rwanda, Uganda, Somalia, Sudan, Haiti, Afghanistan—disease-riddled, poverty-crushed, genoci-dal places, valleys where death, and not just its shadow, stalks and gloats and plunders.

Adam takes photos, interviews survivors, talks to perpetrators, speaks with field workers. He's met a man whose family home, passed down through many generations, was burned to the ground before his eyes. He's met a nine-year-old boy without legs, his young flesh bro-caded with shrapnel. He's met a nine-year-old boy who had killed and killed, and whose eyes showed it. He's met a woman who was forced to watch her husband and sons be tortured to death, and afterward she couldn't stop seeing it, saw it even in her sleep. He's met a woman whose baby died, bony and fly-flecked and listless, in her weary arms, and she had nothing left inside her to care.

These are dispatches from hell. They are testaments to huge evil. To list them like this, stark, like items in a warehouse inventory, fails to communicate sufficiently that this is a darkness huge and swarming and dense, icy cold, inky black, impenetrable.

But even there, in places devoid of light, in faces empty of love or hope, Adam has many times caught the scent or strain of some new thing breaking in: gestures of tenderness, acts of sacrifice, overtures of forgiveness, a quiet but solid joy underneath the brokenness. The bleakness of this hell-racked world, first met, has an engulfing, canceling-out power. Yet something, often faint but real, signals to us that this bleakness does not speak the last word.

I know a woman whose husband terribly betrayed her. He engaged in multiple affairs and ruinous gambling escapades that plundered and squandered all their savings. Then he left her destitute with her young children to raise, no support forthcoming. She took a cleaning job to feed herself and her children. One day, scouring a floor, she hit bottom. She was utterly alone, desperately weary.

Kneeling on wet tiles, her entire body suddenly, unexpectedly, filled with light and strength. "I started to sing," she says. "I couldn't help myself. I suddenly knew, with complete certainty, that no matter what happened in my life, everything would be all right."

What could possibly ease her heart at such a moment?

Knowing that this is not all there is.

Hebrews tells us that those who lived by faith "were longing for a better country—a heavenly one. *Therefore God is not ashamed to be called their God, for he has prepared a city for them*" (11:16, emphasis added).

God is proud to be the God of the heavenly-minded.

"God, would You look at her! In spite of everything, she's so hopeful, so trusting. She is a true citizen of heaven."

"Yes, that's My daughter. I'm her Father."

And the opposite must also be true: God is ashamed to be called the God of those who have no such longing. It is an affront and embarrassment to Him when we become so earthly-minded, so consumed by wanting what the world has, so embittered over what it doesn't, so troubled by our circumstances, that we give no thought to what He has prepared for us.

God made us heaven-bent. He put eternity in our hearts, to pierce us, to lure us. Rich and weary both, all the way home.

Does Life Jusify Living?

S everal years ago I did a wedding on the Sunshine Coast of British Columbia, a one-hundred-kilometer stretch of coastland where a wild shoreline of sandy coves and pebble beaches and rocky shoals meets a puzzlework of primeval rain forest and fjordlike escarpments. The coast is dotted with small villages where prawn trappers, beachcombers, artists, and eccentrics dwell. The wedding ceremony took place far above the clawlike curve of a rock harbor, in a wooden Anglican church built into a cleft of the steep mountain slope.

The inside of the church was decorated in wildflowers gathered from the hills and garden flowers garnered from local homes. In the August heat, the sanctuary smelled of lemon oil and cedar. The bride wore a simple but elegant white dress, the groom his own suit.

Accompanying himself on his scratched but rich-toned guitar, a friend of the couple led the congregation in songs of praise to God. The service had a beautiful simplicity to it, like something hand-carved.

The reception was held outdoors on property the bride's family owned, a promontory that jutted out into a harbor, with a large lawn bordered on two sides by rocky shore and blue-green sea. Sailboats crisscrossed out where the breeze cut unhindered over the water. That same breeze, gentle and fragrant, braided its way over us. The guests gathered on the lawn. Laughter. The ping of crystal. The smell of Cajun shrimp frying over hickory coals. The couple, Edenic in their joy, moving among us, speaking and receiving benediction.

The day was perfect.

In the midst of this, I got into a conversation with a young philosophy student, perhaps in his early twenties, tall and healthy and good-looking. He asked me if I really believed all that religious stuff I had spouted back up at the church. I said I did. He smirked. I asked him what he believed.

"I tried your religion for a while," he said, "and I found it's just a burden to carry. You know what I've figured out? Life justifies living. Life is its own reward and explanation. I don't need some pie-in-the-sky mirage to keep me going. This life has enough pleasure and mystery and adventure in it not to need anything else to account for it. Life justifies living."

"Good," I said. "Very good. And I believe you. Today, here, now—feel the warmth of that breeze, listen to the laughter of those people, smell the spiciness of that shrimp cooking, look at the blueness of that sky—yes, today I believe you. What a superb philosophy. Life justifies living! Bravo!

"Only, I'm thinking about someone I met last February. Richard. Richard was forty-four, looked sixty, and had been living on the streets since he was twelve. He was a junkie. To support his habit, he was a male prostitute until he got too old and ugly and diseased for that. Now he had AIDS, and he was dying hard. He came by the church, looking for prayer, money, food, someone to talk to, odd jobs to do. I helped him out a little.

"The last time I saw Richard was on a gray, rainy day in winter. I bought him a bus ticket and put him on the bus. He was going to his mother's home in Calgary. He hadn't spoken with her in almost fifteen years, but he was hoping he could go home to die. Richard and I sat in my car, waiting for the bus. The rain drummed heavy on the hood and made the windshield opaque, and inside the car the windows steamed up with our breath. Richard was weeping, weeping and shaking. Almost incoherent, he sputtered, 'I wish I'd never been born. My whole life has been a mistake. My whole life has been misery.'

"I'm thinking about Richard. And I'm thinking about Ernie. Ernie was a man on the rise. While he was still in his twenties, he was already vice president of a thriving national business. He was tough minded, hard driving, prodigiously skilled, hugely ambitious. He was a superb athlete, a natural at any sport. He had a beautiful wife. They were unable to have children of their own, so they adopted four of them, three from Africa and one from Mexico. On the day the fourth adoption became final, Ernie got the results back from some medical tests he had undergone to account for some dizziness, blurring of eyesight, tingling and numbing in his hands. The tests came back with stunning news: Ernie had multiple sclerosis.

"Two months ago I sat with Ernie. One of his children is selling drugs in Vancouver and is wanted by the police. Another is in a reform school in Oregon, and if he steps out of line even once, he goes to jail. Ernie is now in his early forties. His once powerful and agile body is twisted, rigid, spasmodic, rawboned. His speech is so shattered that it takes me at least three tries to understand the simplest utterance. It takes him half an hour to eat half a sandwich, and after every bite he nearly chokes.

"Yes, I'm thinking about Richard and Ernie. And I have a question about your philosophy. How exactly do I explain to them that life justifies living?"

The young philosophy student had no response. He said he'd have to think about it and get back to me. I gave him my address and asked him to write me when he came up with something. I never heard from him.

Because life does not justify living.

Eternity does.

PART II

HEAVEN-STRUCK: SEEING THINGS UNSEEN

FIVE

MORE THAN WE ASK OR IMAGINE

Huckleberry Finn didn't think much of heaven.

In the opening chapter of Mark Twain's classic *The Adventures of Huckleberry Finn,* Huck is living with the spinster Miss Watson, a starchy, priggish, crabbed old bone-rack bent on his reform. She's going to knock the wildness out of him and stuff him full of manners. Her principal weapon is religion. She bludgeons him with Bible verses. She threatens him with hell. And she coaxes him with heaven. In his streetwise, cocky, cockeyed way, Huck tells us what he thinks of that:

> She went on and told me all about the good place. She said all a body would have to do there was go around all day long with a harp and sing, forever and ever. So I didn't think

much of it.... I asked her if she reckoned Tom Sawyer would go there, and she said, not by a considerable sight. I was glad about that, because I wanted him and me to be together.[10]

So I didn't think much of it.

I assume that you're like me: I can get itchy-skinned and scratchy-throated after an hour or so of church. I can get distracted and cranky when it goes too long. My feet ache, my backside numbs, my eyes glaze, my mind fogs, my belly growls. I find myself fighting back yawns, and then not fighting them back, letting them gape and roar, a signal to my oppressors: *Let my people go.*

And I'm the pastor.

Is heaven *church forever*?

The popular images we have of heaven only make it worse. A long tradition in art, both classical and pop, has depicted it as the playground of plump, porcelain-skinned cherubs, flitting about on stubby wings or lolling about on downy clouds, plucking harps, singing in sweet, trilling falsettos. Everything is soft, wispy, dainty, pastel, languid. And this is supposed to inspire us.

So I didn't think much of it.

I have an ambition. I want to recover something that has been almost completely buried under the accumulation of two thousand years of false ideas. I want to restore something that, from the tampering and mauling of countless hands, from the blowing and wheezing of countless pulpits, has been so damaged that it's unrecognizable.

I want to render a true picture of heaven.

If we are going to become heavenly-minded, we need a vision of heaven worthy of the effort. If heaven is what the stereotypical portraits of it make it out to be—the chubby angels, the fluffy clouds, the chamber music, the endless church—I'm no more interested in it than Huck Finn is. The only thing that vision of heaven inspires is boredom—or, worse, dread.

Here's the good news: That depiction of heaven misses it entirely. Our clichéd ideas about heaven cannot in the least account for the lives of people like King David, Peter, Paul, John, and a long lineage of Christian martyrs and missionaries, all of them so enthralled with heaven, so ravished by it, that they dared all for it. Have any believers, anywhere, ever worked in a leprosarium or burned at the stake or been devoured by lions because images of doll-like cherubs danced in their heads?

Heaven must be more than we ask or imagine.

Here's the bad news: Although my ambition is to render a true picture of heaven, I'm a poor artist. My drawings are a mess of chicken scratch and thumb smudge. When I try to render some reality in line drawing—the face of one of my children, a vase full of freshly clipped tulips, a wave crashing on a wild jut of rock—it comes out skewed in proportion, both sparse and murky in detail. One night I was playing a game of picture charades with my two daughters. I tried to draw a needle pulling thread. Sarah looked at it, quizzical, and asked, "Is it a paint brush?" "No," Nicola retorted. "It's a heron."

I struggle to render a true picture of heaven in much the same way

I struggle, with my half-baked art skill, to render a true picture of a needle pulling thread.

But here's the surprise: In some ways the creation itself struggles, beneath the weight of its own brokenness and ours, to render a true picture of heaven. "For the creation was subjected to frustration…in hope that the creation itself will be liberated from its bondage to decay and brought into the glorious freedom of the children of God" (Romans 8:20–21). Earthly things are broken copies. The things below are less real, less alive, less solid than the things above: a two-dimensional portrait, static and piecemeal, of an Original that is living and dynamic, four- (or five- or six-) dimensional. Here we only see through a glass darkly.

One Sunday I wanted to demonstrate this for my church. I put an acetate on the overhead projector and then drew a face, a woman's face, heart-shaped, with a dark sheaf of hair framing it. I drew her shoulders, soft and slightly drooping, and a line stretching at shoulder height on either side of her, depicting a landscape horizon. I sketched in her facial features. For her mouth, I drew a thin line slightly curving up, a crimp.

"What is this?" I asked.

"A cat," someone said.

"A woman," someone else said.

"Yes! Good!" I said. "But not just any woman. A famous woman. Who?"

"Your mother," someone said.

"Queen Elizabeth," someone else said.

"Madonna."

"You're all wrong," I said. "Dead wrong. What's the matter with you people? Can't you see that this is the *Mona Lisa*?"

Laughter.

"Why is not one of you in awe, burning with covetousness, plotting how you might, the moment my back is turned, smuggle this out and sell it to an art dealer?"

"Because you're a lousy artist," someone said.

True. Ruefully true. I've told you that already. I had drawn only a shabby copy, a broken shadow, of *Mona Lisa*.

Earth is stunningly beautiful. God has made everything beautiful in its time (see Ecclesiastes 3:11). The fragile petal of a flower, the green curve of a pear, the cool glide of silk on silk, the playful or mournful music of birdsong, the love of a good man or a good woman—all these things are heartrendingly lovely and irreplaceably valuable. Their beauty and value is beyond what we ever could have imagined had we never seen or touched or heard them. Earth is to be treasured and kept well. But it is not the pearl of great price. And it likely bears the same resemblance to the Original that my scratchy doodle bears to da Vinci's *Mona Lisa*.

Heaven must be more than we can ask or imagine.

Jesus strongly suggested that it is.

Preparing for His death, Jesus looks at His distraught followers and says, "Do not let your hearts be troubled. Trust in God; trust also in me" (John 14:1). Within hours He will be betrayed, handed over to men who will shove him and mock him, beat him and kill him. In fear, in bewilderment, these very followers will scatter and hide. But here is Jesus, serene, clear-minded, telling them not to let their hearts be troubled. Why? What does He give as the basis for trust? What does He promise as the source of their consolation?

We might have expected that at this moment, the night before His death, Jesus would remind His disciples of His coming resurrection: *Do not let your hearts be troubled. Trust in God; trust also in Me. Because in three days, I will be up from the grave, triumphant, defiant, on the loose.* Or we might have expected Him to give them a preview of what God's Spirit would accomplish through them: *Do not let your hearts be troubled. Trust in God; trust also in Me. Because when the Spirit comes upon you in power, you are going to stand before kings and rulers and stand down devils and armies, and one day even mighty Rome will be nothing, and the church will be over all the earth.*

But that's not what He promises them. This is: "In my Father's house are many rooms…. I am going there to prepare a place for you. And if I go and prepare a place for you, I will come back and take you also to be with me that you may be where I am" (John 14:2–3).

He inspires them with heaven.

The apostle Paul does the same. He confesses that life sometimes nearly overwhelms him. "We are hard pressed on every side…," he says, "struck down…always being given over to death." Look, he says, face it: There is a stony hardness to life, an unyielding brutality in it. Still he concludes, "We do not lose heart." Why? "For our light and momentary troubles are achieving for us an eternal glory that far outweighs them all" (2 Corinthians 4:8–9, 11, 16–17).

He inspires them with heaven.

The writer of Hebrews does it too. Writing to a disheartened, potentially wayward congregation, he crowns his exhortation with a list of the heroes of the faith, men and women who risked much, sacrificed much, accomplished much on this earth. What kept them keeping on? "They were longing for a better country—a heavenly one" (Hebrews 11:16).

He inspires them with heaven.

Does anyone honestly think that the idea of heaven that lies behind the church's myriad stories of faith and daring, endurance and sacrifice, is nothing more than pillowy clouds, plinky music, and pudgy angels?

Heaven must be more than we ask or imagine.

So how does Scripture draw heaven, so that it will draw us?

Revelation 21 describes walls of jasper, a foundation of topaz and sapphire and emerald, gates of pearl, a street of gold (vv. 18–21). But these are suggestive as much as descriptive. Indeed, Paul describes heaven as indescribable: "No eye has seen, no ear has heard, no mind has conceived what God has prepared for those who love him" (1 Corinthians 2:9).

This isn't an evasion on Paul's part—a rhetorical ploy to conceal his own ignorance. He himself had a vision of heaven in which he was "caught up to the third heaven...caught up to paradise...heard inexpressible things, things that man is not permitted to tell" (2 Corinthians

12:2, 4). It's not that Paul has not glimpsed or tasted heaven. It is, rather, that heaven is beyond his, or any, earthly powers or human freedom to speak about directly.

That's why the biblical grammar of heaven is dense with analogy and simile: Heaven is *like* such and such, it *resembles* so and so, it *has the appearance of* thus and such. Revelation describes the New Jerusalem, the heavenly city, *as* a "bride beautifully dressed for her husband" and *as* a "city of pure gold," while its great street of pure gold is *like* "transparent glass" (Revelation 21:2, 18, 21).

Taken literally, these images only puzzle us. Besides being hard to picture individually, when combined, the images jostle one another, jumble together, almost cancel one another out: *A city of pure but transparent gold that looks like a bride in her tiara and gown?* John, I think, ransacked language and wrested imagination to try to enfold what he saw in familiar words and pictures.

Our attempt to picture heaven has sometimes been compared to twin infants inside the darkness of their mother's womb. They talk about a world outside. They've heard rumors.

One infant says to the other that just beyond the darkness, beyond the thin walls of this cramped place, is dazzling light. It reflects and refracts a billion shades of color and makes visible a vast and astonishing world. There are towering mountains, girdled with millions of trees, crowned with a blinding whiteness. There is a sky, sometimes brilliant blue, other times filled with great white shifting shapes, at still other times a cauldron of grays or an inkwell of blackness flecked with countless tiny sparks. There are immense oceans, darkly raging or glassy smooth. There are creatures of every description above and on and under the earth, large and small, crawling and leaping, soaring and burrowing, diving and slithering, singing, roaring, howling, chattering.

The other infant listens, incredulous, and finally says, "Nah. You're making all this up. There's nothing out there, and if there is, it's probably pretty much like things in here."

In the darkness of the womb, in the limits of an infant's imagination, how could anyone conceive of such wonders? How could anyone picture a giraffe, a waterfall, a ladybug, a zinnia?

That's our predicament. We're the earth-bound trying to become the heavenly-minded. We're struggling to awaken a deep hunger for that which *no eye has seen, no ear has heard, no mind has conceived.* In that sense, we, still earth-bound, can know no more about the world beyond than the two infants, still womb-bound, can know about this world.

But there's hope for us. The Bible says that heaven is grasped by faith, seen with spiritual eyes. "Now faith is being sure of what we hope for," says the writer of Hebrews, *"and certain of what we do not see"* (Hebrews 11:1, emphasis added). "We live by faith," Paul says *"not by sight"* (2 Corinthians 5:7, emphasis added). And after Paul says that no eye has seen, no ear heard, no mind conceived what God has prepared for those who love Him, he says this: "but God has revealed it to us by his Spirit" (1 Corinthians 2:10).

To be heavenly-minded means that we grasp heaven not through the faculties of sight, but through something deeper: by the Spirit and by faith. Daniel Brown, author and pastor, gives a helpful analogy. He could show us, he says, a photograph of his friends, and you'd literally see what they look like. And yet you'd still know almost nothing about them: their quirks, their virtues, the way they move, the timbre and inflection of their voices, their ways with others. A mere physical representation of people is perhaps the least interesting and least informative thing about them. The deeper things about friends are grasped by something other than sight. Similarly, a mere "picture" of heaven tells us almost nothing about it. To really grasp heaven, we must perceive it by faculties other than sight. It is revealed by the Spirit and by faith.[11]

So what do the Spirit and faith reveal about heaven?

Let me back up.

We are born with two impulses. These jostle each other from womb to grave. They make us constantly restless, anxious, weary, cranky.

The first impulse is *to go beyond*. It is to capture some virgin newness, some pristine creation—to fling out wide to the horizons, make a stomach-fluttering leap into the unknown. We seek novelty. We hunger for new beginnings. We crave discovery, conquest, adventure—to find that which has never yet been seen. This impulse often atrophies into escapism.

The second impulse is *to go home*. It is to recapture some unspoiled origins, some unchanging sameness—to dig back down to the bedrock, curl back into the womb. We cherish the familiar. We long for the way we were. We seek safety, domesticity, serenity—to find again that which we've lost. This impulse often calcifies into nostalgia.

To go beyond. To go home. Philosophers and psychiatrists diagnose these opposing impulses as, on the one hand, the desire for self-transcendence—to get past the natural, the habitual, to break out of being who we are. We're bored with ourselves, and want to get outside ourselves. *We want to go beyond.* On the other hand, these contrary impulses represent a desire for self-fulfillment—to get back to nature, to connect again with who we truly are. We're in exile from ourselves and long to return. We're estranged from ourselves and want to be rejoined. *We want to go home.* On earth, not only do these impulses war against one another, but neither impulse is ever satisfied.

The impulse to go beyond makes us feel perpetually bound. We're held back. With every new step we take toward the horizon, the farther away it moves. It's what the writer of Ecclesiastes felt: "I denied myself nothing my eyes desired; I refused my heart no pleasure.... Yet when I surveyed all that my hands had done and what I had toiled to achieve, everything was meaningless, a chasing after the wind" (Ecclesiastes 2:10–11).

And yet the impulse to go home makes us feel perpetually exiled. Home forever eludes. We return to the place where we grew up, the high school we went to, the little church where we were married. But we don't see whatever it is we're looking for. It's gone. We only hear it, faraway and haunting.

Why won't we be bored in heaven? Because it's the one place where both impulses—to go beyond, to go home—are perfectly joined and totally satisfied. It's the one place where we're constantly discovering—where everything is always fresh and the possessing of a thing is as good as the pursuing of it—and yet where we are fully at home—where everything is as it ought to be and where we find, undiminished, that mysterious something we never found down here. All that has held us back here on earth—the weariness, the fear, the dullness, the brevity, the poverty—vanishes. And this lifelong melancholy that hangs on us, this wishing we were someone else somewhere else, vanishes too. Our craving to go beyond is always and fully realized. Our yearning for home is once and for all fulfilled. The *ahh!* of deep satisfaction and the *aha!* of delighted surprise meet, and they kiss.

What will *that* be like? We can only guess. *No eye has seen, no ear has heard, no mind has conceived what God has prepared for those who love Him.* Heaven will be surpassingly, abundantly more than all we ask or imagine.

William M. Dyke became blind when he was ten. When he was in his early twenties and attending graduate school in England, he met the daughter of a British admiral, and they fell in love and decided to marry. But before he agreed to give his daughter's hand in marriage, the admiral insisted that William submit to what was at that time a risky surgery to restore his sight. William agreed, but he also had a condition: He did not want the gauze removed from his eyes until the moment he met his bride at the altar. He wanted her face to be the first thing he beheld on their wedding day.

The surgery took place. The wedding day was set. William's father led his son to the front of the church, and the bride's father led her down the aisle. As she came, William's father stood behind his son and unwound the gauze from his eyes. No one knew if the surgery had been successful. When William's bride stood before him, the last strand of gauze was pulled away, and he was face-to-face with his bride. He stood there speechless, and everyone waited, breathless. And then he spoke: "You are more beautiful than I ever imagined."

One day that will happen to us, only the roles will be reversed. "Now we see but a poor reflection in a mirror," Paul says; "then we shall see face to face. Now I know [Him] in part; then I shall know [Him] fully, even as I am fully known" (1 Corinthians 13:12). One day, the Bride of Christ, near blind now, will stand before her Bridegroom at the Wedding Feast, and the veil will be removed, the scales will fall away, and we will see Him face-to-face and know Him even as we are fully known.

And He will be more beautiful than we ever imagined.

Six

WHO WANTS TO GO TO HEAVEN?

W ho wants to go to heaven?"

The Sunday school teacher put that question to her classroom of boys and girls one day. All the children shot their hands into the air. Except Johnny. He sat there, wavering, sullen, puzzled.

"Johnny?" the teacher said. "Do you *not* want to go to heaven?"

"Well, I guess I do," he said, glum as a caught truant.

"Then why didn't you put up your hand?"

"My mom made chocolate cake for dinner tonight. I was really hoping to have some."

—⁓—

What do the Spirit and faith reveal about heaven? What is heaven *like,* that Johnny—or any of us—should want to go there?

Heaven exists beyond time and space. It exists in the infinite and eternal. We know, for obvious reasons, little about infinity and eternity. But we do know this: All the rules change.

In the Bible we get little glimpses of that—the way the rules change. Consider, for example, the biblical promise that in heaven we *all* receive crowns. There we all are—you, me, curmudgeonly Uncle Willard, saintly and eccentric Aunt Myrtle, Mother Teresa, the repentant thief—each sporting a crown. On earth, the value of something usually increases with scarcity. Pennies are nearly worthless, not just because of their face value, but because of their ubiquity. But if all the pennies on earth were destroyed except one…ah, how valuable that one would be! Earthly value hinges on scarcity.[12]

So what value is a crown if everyone has one?

The best answer is that in heaven the rules change. Value increases on the basis not of scarcity, but of abundance. The more crowns, the more they're worth.

In heaven we move beyond the scale of comparison as well. Scales of comparison are central to earthly values. Earthly things possess a quality of *better* or *worse.* Bach is better than Rachmaninoff, we might say. Or any music is better than country-and-western. Or Gardenburgers are better than Boca Burgers. Earth is inconceivable without scales of comparison.

But in heaven everything exists in its infinite degree, without being better or worse. Everything is what it is and as it ought to be. Everything reposes in the fullness of perfection. And so we will receive rewards in heaven, some more than others, but it is inconceivable that we will feel envy or jealousy toward one another, hold grudges, nurse regrets.[13] We will each display a uniqueness of personality— Revelation says that every person who overcomes will receive from God a white stone with a new name written on it, known only to that person (see Revelation 2:17)—but I imagine that this uniqueness will exist without a hint of oddity or a twinge of feeling alone. We will experience the deepest depths and highest heights of intimacy and yet suffer no loss of self.

The great American theologian Jonathan Edwards had a marvelous image to explain all this. He said that in heaven we are like vessels of varying size. You might have the capacity of an ocean tanker. I might only have the capacity of a saltshaker. But in heaven, every inch and ounce of who we are is perfected and totally filled. Not one grain more of joy, peace, love could be crammed into you.[14] In heaven, every last thing will be filled to the utmost: all is well, and all manner of things will be well.

Heaven is also the meeting place of perfect rest and perfect work. Here again we brush up against an idea that is hard to render in the lexicon of earth. Work and rest to us seem an ocean apart, a canceling out of each other. Just as you can't physically—or even, I suppose, mentally or emotionally—be in Canada and India at the same time, so you can't both be working and resting at the same time. Each requires a different set of poses, intentions, mindsets. Each calls for its own unique pattern of relinquishment and embrace.

We work and we rest fitfully, finding dissatisfaction in both. Our rest is seldom restful; our work rarely fruitful. This is part of our fallenness: We were made to find a fullness in both work and rest, but sin ruptured that, and now "by the sweat of your brow you will eat your food" (Genesis 3:19). Work was once Edenic—a planting and harvesting and naming of creation in the garden—but is now at times demonic, a wrestling of things into and out of the stony, thorny earth. Work embitters more than it fulfills.

It is, for example, a near Herculean task to keep up morale in a workplace. In even the best of work environments, the tendency—the natural state toward which things atrophy—is to become hard-bitten, complacent, bone-weary, gossipy. Sloth, the ancient enemy of the heart, is viral in most workplaces, airborne, mixed in with the water in the watercooler. And what do I do with my own sore feelings and sour attitudes, my own sense of being overworked and undervalued?

It's a lifelong dilemma. But heaven is utterly restorative in both work and rest. The Bible depicts the reward of heaven as both a granting of work and a bestowal of rest: The faithful servant is simultaneously given more jobs to do and yet invited to enjoy the perfect Sabbath (see Hebrews 4; Luke 19:11–26).

I said that heavenly things like this are hard to render in earth's grammar, but maybe not impossible. Imagine a time when you did a good work. You were exhilarated, had a euphoric sense of break-through and accomplishment. You felt an honest pride in a task well done. You were thankful and humble all at once. You experienced community. Others gave heart and soul to the work. You needed one another. You told each other so.

And imagine a time of good rest. You felt completely relaxed and restored. No worries troubled your waking or your sleeping. You had nothing you had to do and were free for anything you chose. You could fish or sleep or read or garden. The tenseness and tiredness in you vanished. You began to think clearly, pray freely, play joyfully. You entered deeply into fellowship and worship, into silence and laughter, and found a healing rhythm for all of it. You experienced *shalom,* the flourishing re-creative vitality of God's breath moving through you.

Imagine now those two things joined seamlessly together, every flaw in them removed, and the whole never fading.

Heaven.

Earth has its comforts. There are sources, deep and true, of replenish-ment and consolation. There are ways God gives back sevenfold the years the locusts have devoured. More than once I've witnessed not just suffering on a Jobian scale, but restoration on that scale too: "The LORD blessed the latter part of Job's life more than the first" (Job 42:12).

I think of my good friend Eugene. Eugene drove home one day to find his house cleaned out. His wife had left and taken their two-year-old daughter, Heather, with her. All she left was a note. She had been having an affair with his best friend, and she had gone to be with him.

Eugene suffered pain so great that, had not the numbness of shock also come over him, it would have pulled him to pieces. His wife and daughter, along with the man she stole off with, had vanished, leaving no forwarding address. Every night for months, Eugene drove through the city streets, going to every place he thought they might be. His search was in vain. After each attempt, he would go home to a cold house, desolate, and fall on his face and weep and beg God.

Finally, Eugene found them. His wife refused to come back. Through some legal maneuvers, she gained exclusive custody of their daughter, Heather, who was then four. The man she had run off with adopted Heather. They never told her of Eugene's existence. When she was eight, Heather's mother died, and his last link with his daughter snapped. Eugene lost his little girl.

On a shelf, Eugene keeps a photograph of Heather and himself, taken a day before he last saw her. He is young, and sad. She is a small girl in a red jacket, her hair swept over her face by the wind. She looks puzzled, the way children do when they know something's wrong but don't know what it is. In a matter of hours, they would be separated. For almost twenty years. Every day for those nearly twenty years, Eugene prayed for her.

But the Lord blessed the latter part of his life more than the first.

In time, Eugene met a beautiful lady, a mother with two girls, who had been through their own Jobian trials. They married and adopted a son. They have had years of good health and financial prosperity.

They moved into and renovated a beautiful log home, with a yard sloping down toward gardens edged in brilliant azaleas and rhododendrons and the main windows and deck overlooking an inner harbor, where sailboats and sports boats and yachts come in and out. Their marriage is strong. Their children and grandchildren are thriving. They travel to Maui or California or Kentucky for holidays. They have many friends who would do anything for them, and they would do anything for their friends.

A few years ago, on Eugene's fiftieth birthday, Heather came back. She found Eugene and wrote to him, and she came back. She lives hundreds of miles away, but they have extended visits with each other several times a year. She's become part of his life, part of his family. Eugene's wife and she are now friends; Heather calls her "Mom," and often the two of them will stay up late into the night and talk about anything, everything, while Eugene, who loves his sleep, shuffles off to bed.

"Good night, honey," he says to her.

"Good night, Dad," she says.

The second Christmas after Heather came back, she shyly showed him her credit card.

"What's this?" he asked.

"Look at the name," she said.

She had changed her last name. It was the same as his.

The Lord blessed the latter part of his life more than the first.

But we've all lived long enough to know that, after suffering, something is lost, irretrievable, and something lingers, inexpugnable.

Some part of us is a graveyard, a wasteland, haunted by memories that won't quite lie to rest.

So a deep pain remains for Eugene and his daughter. Something is always missing. There are conversations they never had and never can have. There are all the years that his daughter went to bed, maybe sucking a thumb and clutching a favorite blanket, when he was not there to read her a story, tuck her in, kiss her. He didn't get to teach her how to ride a bicycle. He wasn't there to look stern and menacing and hide his trembling inside the night she went on her first date. He wasn't there to tell her about God—His infinite bigness and yet the way He becomes small—and he wasn't there to take her to church and hold her hand as they sang "Great Is Thy Faithfulness," and now she has little interest in either God or church. He missed all that, and she did too, and they can't get it back.

How is it, then, that in heaven "there will be no more death or mourning or crying or pain, for the old order of things has passed away" (Revelation 21:4)? *No more death or mourning or crying or pain?* Our sorrow has as much to do with remembered suffering as it does with present suffering. Indeed, most human suffering is cumulative, a lifetime's worth of losses and misses, heartaches and hardships, cruel words uttered and tender words withheld, all piled up and rotting.

So how can there be no more sorrow in heaven? What is the "old order of things" that passes away? Is it that our memories themselves are erased and that all the pain that ambushed us and all the joy that fled us on earth, all the wrong we've done and had done to us, simply slip into a vast sea of forgetting? Or is it that we get divine per-

spective on all these things, with God's transcendent power and consoling depths of understanding—an "aha, so that's what God was up
to" revelation?

Perhaps.

But maybe it's different from that.

Maybe in heaven all our losses are not forgotten. Maybe they're
returned. Maybe all the broken and strewn parts of ourselves come
back, more alive and connected than they've ever been. But regardless
of that, this one thing is true: Heaven is where our inescapable sense
of loss and incompleteness is overcome. It is the one thing large
enough to answer our deepest longings and console our deepest
griefs. Our hunger for perfect justice and perfect mercy and perfect
joy and perfect peace—all is met there.

Maybe, just maybe, the sorrow is not forgotten, or bathed in the
light of perfect understanding. Maybe all of it, every last shred of it, is
redeemed, given back.

And Eugene gets to tuck Heather into bed, and sing her a lullaby.

There's more. I could talk about the new heart and transformed mind
and spiritual body we'll receive in heaven. I could talk about being co-
heirs with Jesus and getting to reign with Him. I could talk about the
unhindered and uncorrupted intimacy we'll experience with one
another or the joy of our reunion with those who have gone before, a
joy infinite in scope, eternal in duration.

I could talk about all that, but I don't want to miss the best and the most important thing about heaven, the one thing that makes heaven heavenly and apart from which heaven is just another theme park.

John was granted a glimpse of heaven. And though he describes, as best he can with the rough tool of language, the creatures and geography and architecture of heaven, that isn't what captivates his heart and mind. This is:

> I looked, and there before me was a door standing open in heaven.... At once I was in the Spirit [these things are spiritually discerned], and there before me was a throne in heaven *with someone sitting on it.*
>
> Then I saw a Lamb, looking as if it had been slain, standing in the center of the throne. (Revelation 4:1–2, emphasis added; 5:6)

Later, John tells us that the presence of this Someone is the most amazing thing about heaven:

> "Now the dwelling of God is with men, and he will live with them. They will be his people, and God himself will be with them and be their God."
>
> He who was seated on the throne said, "I am making everything new!... I am the Alpha and the Omega, the Beginning and the End." (Revelation 21:3, 5–6)

The most important thing about heaven is God, revealed in Jesus Christ.

We're going to see God. We will be given eyes to behold what angels fear to look upon, and through Christ the boldness and privilege to draw near. And however we conceive that, or fail to conceive it, it is a glory and a joy beyond our wildest imaginings. Even if nothing else is true about heaven, God dwells there in the fullness of His splendor, and that alone gives heaven its worth. God alone makes heaven heavenly.

The picture that became *Life* magazine's photo of the decade for the 1980s isn't technically all that good. It's a bit blurry. It lacks crispness. The colors are weak, a bit smudged.

But the photo didn't win for its artistic merit. It was chosen for its subject matter. It's a photo of one of the Iranian hostages returning home. The hostages, fifty-two in all, were kept in stone cells in Tehran for 444 days. They were poorly fed, mentally tortured, beaten with fists and boots and clubs. No one knew if they would get out alive. The American people rallied to support them.

Tony Orlando had a hit song then, "Tie a Yellow Ribbon 'Round the Old Oak Tree." It's a sentimental ballad about a man who wants to come home but doesn't know if he's still welcome. So he writes home. *I'll pass by,* he says, *and if you still want me, tie a yellow ribbon around the oak tree by the house.* The American people seized on that as their emblem, their banner of hope. All through the long wait, all over

America, people tied yellow ribbons around trees, lampposts, flag and telephone poles. They laced them to their car antennas, wore them in their hair, hung them from the door.

The photo. It's of a man, one of the hostages, crossing the airport tarmac in Germany. He's a free man. His daughter, seeing him, has broken out from the crowd waiting for the returning prisoners. She has run, fast and hard. She is maybe eight years old. She wears a yellow dress. Behind her, tied around her waist, is a huge lacy ribbon, bright yellow as sunshine. The photographer has caught her leaping into her daddy's arms, his embrace enfolding her.

It's the look on his face that gets you. He is permanently wonder-struck, joy-filled, weeping with the sheer power of thankfulness.

Heaven is *that* forever.

Who wants to go to heaven?

SEVEN

HEAVEN
CAN'T WAIT

M y parents said we'd go to Disneyland. Next year, for sure. The best part was that they planned to take us out of school and fly us down in the dead of winter. We lived in a mill town in northern Canada, where winter was endless and cruel. Daylight was arthritic in arriving, nimble in escape. The sun, when we saw it, was a pale, thin thing slipping along the earth's rim. It made a swift but timid showing, and then the enormous darkness swallowed it whole again. Stay inside if you can. If you can't, if some desperate need drives you outside, dress in thick layers: down, fleece, wool. No cotton. Leave no skin exposed. The coldness can scald like boiling oil and peel you down to the bones.

But we were going to Disneyland. And flying—soaring miles above the earth in a great gleaming jet whose seats were in rows as wide as a movie house and where pretty ladies in pantsuits served Coke for free. The highest I'd been in the air before, if this counts, was in seventh grade, when I got to go to the top floor of the ten-story telephone company building in downtown Prince George.

But now we were going to fly—and to Disneyland. My brother and I were delirious with impatience. We had seen a television show about the place: dream castles spinning their banner-fluttering turrets skyward, a band of wisecracking bears plucking banjos and thumping washtubs, a tree house just like the one where the Swiss Family Robinson held off the pirates, an island just like the one where Tom Sawyer and Huck Finn hid from Aunt Molly. We were agog. Joy ached in us.

We saw ourselves there, light-footed in shorts and tank tops while our ice-bound schoolmates, mummified in winter wear, trudged through snowdrifts and skittered across ice fields. We'd laugh, our arms spread winglike, as the roller coaster swooped through another hairpin turn coming down the Matterhorn. Laugh as we wove a skiff between exploding cannonballs among the Pirates of the Caribbean. Laugh as we darted in a submarine through waters filigreed with coral, teeming with sharks. I even wanted to see those mechanical talking birds that bobbed in unison and trilled in harmony. We'd laugh then too.

We never went.

There was always some reason, but it usually came down to money. Either there was not enough, or, if there was a little extra, something came up: The car broke down or my grandma got sick and my mother had to fly back East, or an accumulation of any number of sundry things. So Disneyland got put off and put off. At fourteen, I finally realized that it was a chimera, a unicorn in the garden, the thing you dreamed but never saw in the waking realm.

I finally did go to Disneyland. I was thirty-five. I was at a church conference and bored, and I was two blocks away from Walt's fabled kingdom. So I went. I had two deacons and a youth pastor in tow. It was okay. But the place was a little worn down, I was a little worn out, and—I told you this already—I was thirty-five and with deacons. The mechanical birds were twittering annoyances. The mechanical bears were more slapdash than slapstick. The Swiss Family Robinson tree house was being dismantled, and the Matterhorn was closed for repairs.

A melancholy hung over the whole thing. It was like arriving at the end of a birthday party, when the cake is a mound of crumbs, the wrapping paper all tatters, the children cranky and weary. It was like coming at the end of the parade with the streets empty of people but strewn with litter—spilled popcorn and cotton candy sticks and handbills announcing Boy Scouts and dance classes. I did shake hands with Mickey Mouse, but the magic just wasn't in it. I understood perfectly then what Solomon meant: "Hope deferred makes the heart sick" (Proverbs 13:12).

"There are two kinds of preaching that people won't put up with," Fred Craddock once said. "Bad preaching, and good preaching."

When preaching is lame, flat, zeal-less, mawkish, heretical, it des-iccates people, withers them up. But when preaching is robust, feisty, zealous, substantial, orthodox, it slays people, overwhelms them.

I think that's true of writing also. Write poorly, you steal something from your reader. Write well, you give a gift maybe too much to bear.

If I've written poorly here, I've made heaven less real, chimerical. I've stolen from you. But if I've written well, I've made heaven—well, heavenly. That's what I've wanted to do: to take what may have been for you just a faint thirst or a quaint curiosity and stir it into a wild hunger. Truly taste heaven, and you're like a fox who has raided the henhouse—you won't be satisfied with anything less.

But hope deferred makes the heart sick. For many of us, heaven's a long way off, as far as we know. Yes, one day we'll be with God—no more pain or sorrow or fear. And one day we'll be like God—no more sin and pettiness and selfishness. But what about getting through the pain and sorrow and fear of this week? What about the sin and petti-ness and selfishness entangling us today? What if right now we're penniless, sick, heartbroken, goaded and shaken by temptation?

Heaven help us.

But how? How does heaven help us—here, now, buried in the thick of trouble, crushed beneath the weight of grief? Yes, of course, the thought of heaven puts all trouble and grief in perspective. But to talk of heaven in the midst of despair and tragedy is perhaps like prais-ing fire to a half-frozen man or extolling sleep to an insomniac. It's like telling starving people in the Sudan that there's food in America. *See, look, here's a picture. This is Mr. Mike's. And this is Red Lobster. And...*

It doesn't help. It only makes it worse.

Here's a single mother. She subsists on welfare. Two of her children are sick: In the day, they're listless and whiny; in the night, each wakes in turn, crying, inconsolable. Her third child is on the cusp of singularly wild-faring adolescence and daily hollers abuse and accusation at her mother, at her siblings. This morning, an eviction notice came in the mail, mixed in with the overdue bills. Tonight will be the fourth time in a row they eat plain spaghetti—with ketchup for sauce—deliberately overcooked to make it more filling. Weariness is in her very marrow.

Go, tell her: "God works all things together for good...."

Or here's a village in India, where an earthquake buckled the ground and all the buildings shook apart. It's been three days, and many bodies still haven't been found, and now everything has to be burned—the bodies, the ruins—to get rid of the odor and prevent disease from breeding in the air. A woman sits on a thin plank of wood that was once the threshold of her home. Brick shards and splintered timber lie all around her in heaps. There's a tightness around her eyes, her mouth. Her face is blank. She holds a blanket, tiny, threadbare, fringed with a silky blue ruffle. She's unmoving, except her right hand. With it, she rubs and rubs a corner of the blanket, over and over, and now and then lifts it to press the blanket to her cheek and just hold it there.

Go, tell her: "Fix your eyes not on what is seen, but on what is unseen. For what is seen is temporal. But what is unseen is eternal."

Or here are New Yorkers on the evening of September 11, 2001,

that day of death and desolation when terrorists hijacked four airlin-
ers and crashed two of them into the twin towers of the World Trade
Center, one into the Pentagon, and one into an uninhabited field in
Pennsylvania. The sky fell; the sun grew dark.

Thousands of people died. Mothers, fathers, children.
Grandparents, uncles, aunts. Neighbors. Best friends. Fellow church-
goers. Corporate CEOs and the old black man who shined their
shoes. Banking magnates and the Guatemalan woman who cleaned
their offices. Bike couriers, scruffy and nimble, delivering the first
round of mail that day. All dead.

One of them was Anne Judge, my brother's good friend from
National Geographic. Adam had been on several photographic expedi-
tions with her, to Greece, Malta, Italy, Spain, Morocco. Whenever he
was in Washington D.C., Adam stayed at the house that she and her
husband, Geoff, owned in Virginia. She had a quicksilver smile and a
raspy, earthy laugh.

On that morning, she had to fly with another colleague on
American Airlines, flight #77, from Washington to Los Angeles. They
were taking, as part of an educational program, a group of school children and their teachers: children whose parents had dressed them in
clean bright clothes for this special trip, kissed them at the airport, and
waved to them as they passed through security. "Be careful. Have fun."

It was a perfect day for flying, clear and crisp, all things washed
by the night's dew, burnished in the early morning light. The air had
an autumn chill, and the grass was almost white with the night's heavy
dew. Anne and her colleague, the children and their teachers boarded

the plane, and then they were off, the earth tumbling away beneath them.

A half hour or so into the flight, things went horribly awry. Five men, wielding plastic knives and waving a red box they claimed contained a bomb, took captive the crew and passengers. One of the men got in the cockpit, made a hairpin turn in the sky, and dove headlong into the Pentagon.

Go, tell Anne's husband, or any of the parents of any one of those children: "Don't lose heart. Your light and momentary troubles are achieving for you a glory that far outweighs them all."

Words, mere words, worthless words, it seems, in the face of such utter catastrophe. A fistful of water flung at a spewing volcano, these. A tin hut built against a typhoon. Even for those of us who have deep convictions about heaven, it can—some days, some weeks, some years—seem a terrible and mocking knowledge, more a taunt than a consolation.

Heaven help us.

But how?

Heaven helps us by giving us a focal point when we look up. "Set your hearts on things above," Paul says, "where Christ is seated at the right hand of God" (Colossians 3:1). Our focal point is *Christ seated at the right hand of God.*

At first blush, this picture turns me cold. Christ seated at the right hand of God? My mind instinctively conjures up an iconic painting in the orthodox tradition, Christ a flattened-down figure, ashen and somber, perched stiffly on an ornate throne, spidery pale hands raised up in a hieratic gesture. He is, it seems, in a sour mood, in an airless room, stifling and chill all at once.

How can I set my mind on this, I wonder, *and how might it help me live with purity and holy vigor and unquenched hope?* How does *this* hold off the wiles of temptation, throw off the weight of sadness, pluck out the claws of terror? How will *this* awaken in me courage and stamina? Is *this* what Stephen saw the day the Sanhedrin dragged him outside, gnashing their teeth, howling their rage, gathering fistfuls of rock? Is *this* what kept him childlike in wonder and forgiveness?

But here I get it wrong: *It is not the image itself that is meant to be our focus.* It is, rather, what the image represents. It's a symbol.

It's a flag.

Nobody is inspired by a flag as a mere physical object, a chunk of colored cloth flapping in the wind from the tip of a pole. As a thing in itself, it inspires nothing—not passion, not loyalty, not pride, not hope. No one would die for it *as a mere thing.* We'd call that insanity.

But many are inspired to acts of servanthood and heroics, even to sacrifice unto death, for what a flag means. Think of your own nation's flag. It stands for many things: your home and your grandparents' home, your schools, your friends, the bakery where you buy hot cross buns at Easter, the children who play in the park where you walk in the evenings. Your nation's flag means all this and more. Many risk or make sacrifice for *that.* We call this patriotism.

The week after the destruction of the World Trade Center, a photo appeared around the world. It is a picture, evocative of the soldiers raising the flag at Iwo Jima, of three firemen raising an American flag to half-mast. The flag is unsullied, brilliant red, white, blue. The three men themselves are bedraggled, stained with soot and dust. The flagstaff is crooked. The backdrop is desolation: a bleak landscape of gray rubble, the broken remains of the World Trade Center. A mountain of smoking ruin. You can see in those men a fierce fixed determination, a holy defiance, a pride of country deeper than sorrow, stronger than fear. You can see a wild hungry hope. That flag is more than a flag. It embodies and distills their deepest loyalties. It commands their highest allegiance.[15]

Christ seated at the right hand of God. Paul is flying the flag. Its power of inspiration lies not in the picture itself, but in what it stands for.

What the image of the seated Christ means is that He is reigning with God in power, justice, and mercy. It means that Christ loves you and that He is personally, passionately involved in conforming you to His image. He is in control, interceding for you before the Father. He is no iconic figure, prim and dour, stiff with scorn. He leaps with joy at the sight of you.

That's what the flag stands for. Set your heart and mind there. Shape and fill your thinking with that.

In the book of Acts we see how this works out in practice. Peter and John have just been roughed up and horsewhipped by the Sanhedrin and sent away with a stern warning: Don't ever talk about Jesus again. On their release, they go and tell the other believers "all that the chief priests and elders had said to them" (Acts 4:23).

What do you usually do when you're in trouble? When things don't turn out as you'd hoped? Panic? Despair? Retaliate? This is what Peter and John do:

> When they heard this, they raised their voices together in prayer to God. "Sovereign Lord," they said, "you made the heaven and the earth and the sea, and everything in them." (Acts 4:24)

They set their hearts and minds on things above, where Christ is seated at the right hand of God. They remember who's really in charge and who loves them.

They fly the flag.

I think Jesus would be puzzled by our preoccupation with heaven as something that is exclusively *hereafter.* "The kingdom of God does not come with your careful observation," Jesus said, "nor will people say, 'Here it is,' or 'There it is,' because *the kingdom of God is within you*" (Luke 17:20–21, emphasis added).

The night before Jesus went to the cross, He shared a meal with His disciples. He taught them many things, more than they could fully grasp at the time. He told them about heaven and said that He was going there to prepare a place for them and that He would come back and take them to be with Him. He washed their feet. After all this, He prayed for them.

It's the prayer that intrigues me. Just before He prayed it, He spoke of the disasters to come and said, "I have told you these things, so that in me you may have peace. In this world you will have trouble" (John 16:33). *In this world you will have trouble.* One way or another, you will have trouble, large or small, intimate or corporate, local or global. The daily annoyances. The cosmic catastrophes. The private sorrows. The national tragedies. No one is exempt. Jesus says, "But take heart! I have overcome the world" (John 16:33).

Then He prays.

After Jesus said this, he looked toward heaven and prayed: "Father, the time has come. Glorify your Son, that your Son may glorify you. For you granted him authority over all people *that he might give eternal life to all those you have given him."* (John 17:1–2, emphasis added)

Jesus Christ has the Father's authority to grant eternal life. None of us can see the kingdom of God except that Jesus ushers us in.

So far, heaven is something *over there, up ahead.*

But Jesus continues:

Now this is eternal life: that they may know you, the only true God, and Jesus Christ, whom you have sent." (John 17:3)

This is eternal life: that they may know You…and know Me.
There is something about heaven and eternity that we have to

grasp, because if we don't, we'll miss everything else. We'll read the music but never sing, study the choreography but never dance.

It's this: Heaven starts now.

Eternity is not primarily a measure of time—chronological time stretched to infinity. It is not first and foremost a place. Eternity is primarily a quality of relationship. It is first and foremost a presence: to *know* God and Jesus Christ.

Eternity begins now.

Christianity's most shocking claim is that Jesus is the only way to God. No one gets to heaven apart from Jesus. No one enters eternal joy apart from Christ. That's our claim. I have seen people react to it with anger, contempt, disgust, incredulity. *How dare you say that! That is so arrogant and narrow and imperialistic.* That reaction might be warranted if heaven were only a place and eternity only a duration of time. But heaven is a unique knowing. It is personal, intimate knowledge, not of some thing, but of Some One—the only true God and Jesus, the one He sent.

This is eternal life.

EIGHT

THE CIRCLE OF NAMING

B y simple definition, you can't live eternally in heaven apart from knowing Jesus Christ, because knowing Jesus Christ is exactly what heaven and eternity is all about.

What does that mean—to *know* the only true God and Jesus Christ?

Helen Keller, blind, deaf, and mute, learned through the patient and loving guidance of Anne Sullivan to communicate, first through touch and then through speech. When Anne first tried to teach her about God, Helen said, "I already know about Him—I just don't know His name."[16]

That's us: born with an instinctive knowledge of God, a knowing that is deeper than language or image, prior to word and picture, but still a vague knowing. It's all shadow, rumor, echo. We don't know His name. That has to be revealed to us. It's not something we can conjure up or figure out on our own. Apart from revelation, God is veiled. "I have *revealed you* to those whom you gave me," Jesus says (John 17:6, emphasis added). Jesus reveals the Father.

But the Father also reveals Jesus. When Peter confessed Jesus as the Christ, Jesus responded: "Blessed are you, Simon son of Jonah, for this was not revealed to you by man, but by my Father in heaven" (Matthew 16:17). Revelation, in substance, is simply Christ revealing the Father and the Father revealing Christ. It is a circle of naming, a compact of divine disclosure: *This is My Son, this is My Father, I am...*

As a boy, I used to watch a show on Canadian television called *Front Page Challenge*. It featured a panel of Canadian luminaries, both guests and regulars. Writer and historian Pierre Burton was usually on, and Betty Kennedy, as well as journalist Gordon Sinclair and, replacing him, Allan Fotheringham. Four in all formed the panel. Then there was a mystery guest—someone of current notoriety in politics or religion or sports or the arts. He or she sat in a booth at the back of the studio, enshrouded in shadow, silhouetted against a spectral blue light. Sometimes, if the shape of the mystery guest was itself noteworthy, the guest was thickly veiled, sometimes even situated off-camera. If the voice was too easily recognizable, it was disguised with a Russian accent or a raw nasal twang. Occasionally, a woman would try to sound like a man.

It was an intellectual whodunit, a pundit's game of cat-and-mouse. The panel would ask the mystery guest questions that only could be answered yes or no. Are you in Canadian politics? "Yes."

Were you involved in the recent parliamentary scandal? "No."

The object was to name the mystery guest within a certain time limit. Often, the panel could. But sometimes, all their shrewd probing and sharp grilling and tireless stone-turning led to dead ends and empty rooms. On those occasions, after the time was up, host Fred Davis would announce—he'd name—the special guest, and the mystery guest would step from the shadows, emerge into the light, and then engage in a freewheeling discussion with the panel.

I know about Him; I just don't know His name.

With God, that has to be revealed every time.

But how? How does Jesus reveal God? It's good for us that Philip asked that very thing:

> "Lord, show us the Father and that will be enough for us."
> Jesus answered: "Don't you know me, Philip, even after I have
> been among you such a long time? Anyone who has seen me
> has seen the Father. How can you say, 'Show us the Father'?
> Don't you believe that I am in the Father, and that the Father
> is in me?" (John 14:8–10)

It is the circle of naming. To know God, you must know Jesus. To know Jesus is to know God.

The knowing that is eternal life is not academic, at least not merely academic. It is both infinitely more and dramatically less than the best theological training can give us.

Paul, of course, openly warns about a different sort of knowing, one that is haughty and cocksure, boasting and taunting. It makes a fetish of esoteric things. It hoards and flaunts secrets. It is lordly and pretentious, smug and scornful. It is quarrelsome, too, always seeking a thinner hair to split, a more subtle shade of distinction to mark out, some quixotic pedantry to quibble over. Those who know in this way are know-it-alls, and yet they know nothing. They are mere idea-mongers, stuffed silly with the latest in intellectual trinkets and gadgets.

This is not the knowing that is the heart of eternal life. That knowing is different. It is personal and intimate, and yet not secretive. It's not buried deep in some gnostic riddle book. It is open for all to see, to hear, to receive—to know.

It is the knowing of recognition.

Not long ago, my family and I flew to Oregon for a weekend speaking engagement I had. On the flight home, we had a nearly four-hour layover at the SeaTac airport. My brother and his family live in Seattle, and they knew we were switching planes at SeaTac. They packed a picnic lunch and came down to meet us. We walked off the plane and into the teeming labyrinth of the airport. People rushing and jostling, running late. People bored and listless, forced to wait. All of them strangers to us.

Then we saw them: my brother, my sister-in-law, my niece and nephew. Family. All the while we were growing up, my brother and I played and fought and explored together. We spent our summers sleeping in our backyard in a tent, which we left up so long that by the end of August, when we folded it up, we had to scrape a layer of hoary mildew from its underside. We spent our winters side by side on the ski slope or the ice rink. We grieved together a runaway dog, a cat hit by a car, a friend who died falling down the steep cutbanks by the river. We rejoiced together in the arrival of our baby sister, born late, just as we were becoming teenagers. We conspired with each other, sometimes tattled on each other. We shared a bedroom for many years. I got his hand-me-downs, until that wasn't cool anymore. We attended each other's graduation ceremonies. We were best man at each other's wedding.

I *know* him.

Our wives are close friends and have probably told each other things that they've never told to anyone else, even to us, their husbands. Our children are best friends. Every year, our families spend a week together, in a cabin on the oceanfront or a houseboat on one of our country's vast cold deep lakes. We walk together, eat together, play Mouse Trap and Rummoli together, read portions of books to each other.

We *know* them.

That's the knowing Jesus invites us into.

But is it even possible to know Jesus this way? If so, how? How do we enter and sustain such intimate knowing? Jesus isn't physically here. God has never shown Himself to me in the way my brother has. We don't share life together quite like that.

Or do we?

When Jesus first told His disciples that He was returning to the Father, He consoled them with the promise of the Holy Spirit. The Spirit is Christ's very presence with us, within us. But there is an essential element to experiencing the Spirit's presence. Jesus gives us the key insight:

> "I have revealed you to those whom you gave me…you gave them to me and they have obeyed your word. *Now they know* that everything you have given me comes from you. For I gave them the words you gave me and they accepted them. *They knew with certainty* that I came from you." (John 17:6–8, emphasis added)

We know the Spirit, and so know Jesus and so know the Father, primarily in one way: by studying, accepting, and obeying the Word of God.

Billy Graham was asked, "If you had to live your life over again, what would you do differently?" He replied:

> One of my great regrets is that I have not studied enough. I wish I had studied more and preached less. People have pressured me into speaking to groups when I should have been studying and preparing. Donald Barnhouse said that if he knew the Lord was coming in three years, he would spend two of them studying and one preaching.[17]

They have obeyed Your word, Jesus said. *Now they know who I am. They accepted Your words,* He said. *And so they knew with certainty who I am.* There is no way to know who Jesus is apart from the acceptance of and obedience to the Word.

Like an ancient glassblower sculpting molten glass into useful and beautiful wares with just His breath, God's Holy Spirit breathed into each word of Scripture, shaping it with fire and wind to one over-arching purpose: so you would *know* God and *know* Jesus. To read the Bible and miss this is to misread it.

Tom Wright tells the story of one man, a prisoner named Jason Richards, who instinctively understood what the Bible is all about:

> I hadn't been long in my sentence and I was very con-fused.... I was carrying an awful lot of guilt. I was looking for answers. I read a lot. I read Buddhism. I read Islam. I started reading the Bible. And the more I read the Scriptures, the more I became aware of God.
>
> I didn't believe in God. I was actually an atheist—or at least I thought I was. But I came to believe that God existed. And the more I became aware of God the more I became aware that I was a sinner—and I got more and more desperate.
>
> Then one night...I opened the Bible at the very first Psalm. I started reading...and when I got to Psalms 50 and 51, I realized that God would forgive me. I didn't know [why Psalm 51 had been written] then. But the thing I knew was, "Save me from bloodguilt, O God, the God who saves me, and

my tongue will sing of your righteousness."

I knew that God would forgive me…. I didn't know anything about Jesus or the Bible or the Church. I just knew. I
read all the rest of the Psalms on my knees—and almost from
that point for me they became psalms of praise. It was like I
was beginning to worship, and I didn't know what worship
was.[18]

Jesus rebuked those who read the Scriptures but didn't fall in
love with Him: "You diligently study the Scriptures because you
think that *by them you possess eternal life*. These are the Scriptures that
testify about me, yet you refuse to come to me to have life" (John
5:39–40, emphasis added). Knowing the Bible is not eternal life;
eternal life is knowing the only true God and knowing Jesus Christ.
But you will only know Christ if you know—and accept and obey—
His Word.

There is fruit of such knowing. The knowing that Jesus calls us to is
so intimate that increasingly it becomes imitation: His life flowing into
us, through us, shaping us from inside out. It is water that soaks all
that's porous in us, fire that burns all that's combustible. It is His life
pressed into our flesh so long that the texture of it imprints us, indelible. You know that you know Jesus because more and more you
become like Jesus.

Jesus Himself is explicit about this:

"Holy Father, protect them by the power of your name—the name you gave me—so that they may be one as we are one.

"I am coming to you now, but I say these things while I am still in the world, so that they may have the full measure of my joy within them.

"As you sent me into the world, I have sent them into the world. For them I sanctify myself, that they too may be truly sanctified. I pray...that all of them may be one, Father, just as you are in me and I am in you. May they also be in us.... I have given them the glory that you gave me, that they may be one as we are one: I in them and you in me. May they be brought to complete unity to let the world know that you sent me and have loved them even as you have loved me.

"I have made you known to them, and will continue to make you known in order that the love you have for me may be in them and that I myself may be in them." (John 17:11, 13, 18–23, 26)

You know that you know Jesus because more and more you become like Him. You rejoice—not with a joy built on the rickety sticks of circumstance, but the joy that is anchored in the bedrock of Truth and Spirit. You love—not with a love that flits and whirls, pleasure-driven, emotion-laced, but the love that is deep-rooted, hard-resolved. You are holy—not with a holiness that is dour and prissy, but the holiness that is fierce, wild, robust. And you seek unity—not a unity that is a thinly-papered truce, a taped-and-stapled-together coalition, but the unity that draws its power and example from the Trinity itself.

This is the unity of deep calling to deep, where the Christ who lives in me seeks out and delights in the Christ who lives in you. Oneness. This is a fruit of Christlikeness that Jesus stresses in His prayer. He emphasizes it because our proneness to divide is deep in our bones.

A Baptist was the lone survivor of a shipwreck. He ended up a castaway on a desert island. Many years later a ship passed, and the crew saw the man's SOS. The ship anchored, and the captain sent some rescuers ashore. The man greeted them.

"Well," he said, "before we leave, let me show you around my island. That building over there is the Baptist church I built when I first arrived. And this over here is my home. And left of that is the shed I constructed to store the produce I cultivated. And next to that is the barn where I keep the animals that I domesticated. And then, way over there, is the Baptist church I built...."

"Wait a minute," one of the rescuers said. "I thought the building back there was the Baptist church you built."

"Oh," the man said, "I don't go to *that* church anymore."[19]

We can get in a snit over just about anything. Most church splits are not about matters of great moral or theological weight. Most are about trivia: too many songs that we don't like sung on Sundays, a squabble over a building proposal that swells into a feud, a debate about the youth group's latest prank that went awry, a deadlock over who's really in charge of the kitchen. I know something of this. I'm a pastor. Well over half of the reasons I've heard for why people leave the church are embarrassingly petty, a case of swallowing camels and straining out gnats.

Jesus says that as we know Him better and become more like Him, we will embody a oneness with other believers that is *just as* the oneness that Jesus and the Father enjoy. Is that possible, or is it just fanciful rhetoric? It is not only possible; it is ultimately inevitable, a holy compulsion larger and stronger than all our factionalism. It's a oneness that does not derive from cultural or genetic sameness—we can look differently, speak differently, have different tastes and back-grounds. It derives, rather, from the fact that Jesus is in you and Jesus is in me. The oneness is simply, deeply, the Spirit of Jesus Christ in me uniting with the Spirit of Jesus Christ in you.

That's why Paul says that we grieve the Holy Spirit within us—we break the Spirit's heart—when we don't cooperate with His work of reconciliation and community. "Make every effort," Paul says, "to keep the unity of the Spirit" (Ephesians 4:3). It's a gift, a finished work, but you and I must make effort—*every* effort—to keep it. "Do not grieve the Holy Spirit of God, with whom you were sealed for the day of redemption. Get rid of all bitterness, rage and anger, brawling and slander, along with every form of malice. Be kind and compassionate to one another, forgiving each other, just as in Christ God forgave you" (Ephesians 4:30–32).

"How good and pleasant it is when brothers live together in unity!" Psalm 133 begins. It concludes with this: "For there the LORD bestows his blessing, *even life forevermore*" (Psalm 133:1, 3, emphasis added).

We can taste heaven now. It's God's intent that we should. But it requires *knowing* Jesus through His Word in such a way that we become more and more like Him, with His joy, His love, His holiness, His oneness in us, flowing through us.

In the 1960s through the '80s, Arthur Burns was chairman of the U.S. Federal Reserve System and the ambassador to West Germany. He was a personal friend and economic counselor to a long line of U.S. presidents. He wielded huge influence.

He was also Jewish. So it was a surprise when in the 1970s he began to show up regularly at a Christian group that met once a week for fellowship and prayer at the White House. He was welcomed. But no one knew quite what to do with him. Week after week, year after year, different people took turns ending the meeting in prayer. But Arthur Burns was never asked to do this.

One day the leader of the group was a newcomer who didn't know Arthur Burns, and at the end of the meeting, he turned to him and asked him if he'd close in prayer. Some of those who had been coming to the meeting for a long time looked askance at each other. What would Burns do?

He never flinched. He stretched out his hands to join hands with the others in the circle. He bowed his head. "Lord," he said, "I pray that You would bring Jews to know Jesus Christ. I pray that You would bring Muslims to know Jesus Christ. Finally, Lord, I pray that You would bring Christians to know Jesus Christ. Amen."[20]

Like a Boy Eavesdropping

The kingdom of heaven is like…" That was one of Jesus' favorite gambits—a sharp goad to rouse apathy, a shiny lure to hook curiosity. Then He'd tell a story. There were so many stories, so many things the kingdom of heaven is like. It is like finding a pearl of staggering beauty and priceless worth in, of all places, a stony field. It is like a mustard seed, small as a pepper flake, but if hidden long enough in the fertile earth, becoming the largest tree, unfolding its magnificence skyward, providing shelter for all who seek it. It is like a banquet, a hullabaloo of feasting and dancing, thronged with beggars and waifs brought in at the last minute, after the invited guests canceled in order to yoke oxen or inspect houses. It is like a man going away on a journey, and then returning unannounced, almost as a prank, surprising the servants. It is like a groom coming for his bride late, almost past waiting for, catching the brides-maids unprepared.

It is like my lunch with Gary and Elaine.

They had been at the church longer than I had. For nine years, they'd run a counseling practice in town—the only distinctly Christian one within a half-hour's drive. People whose lives had been ruptured by grief, plundered by loss, numbed from trauma, waylaid with tragedy, hobbled by cruelty, hamstrung through neglect—people whose fathers had abused them, whose mothers had ignored them, whose spouses had betrayed them, whose children had rejected them, people whose emotional lives could no more be repaired by self-effort than a man with liver failure could be healed by his own dexterity—these were the people they had helped. Families were reconciled. Marriages were reclaimed. Phobias were overcome. The oil of joy was given for ashes, garlands of grace for sackcloth. Gary and Elaine were one of Christ's means of inviting His people into abundant life.

But today, they knew none of it themselves. Today, they were both thin shells, brittle and fragile, roiling on the inside with immense pain. The work at the best of times emptied both of them, but usually in turn, so that the weak one could borrow the other's strength. But not today. Today, they were both empty, weary, despondent. They were at the place where most of the people who came to them were: the last straw, the last ditch, the last hope. Not only had the work ransacked them, but a few weeks earlier, by a single decision made by an anony-mous bureaucrat in a distant government office, a large portion of their revenue had been cut off overnight. Though they had a long list of people wanting to see them, they could no longer keep the practice viable. They would have to close.

Gary and Elaine came into the restaurant smiling. But their smiles were painted on. They were brokenhearted, bleeding on the inside.

We ordered our lunch—watery egg salad sandwiches—and ate it. All the while, they told their story. The telling at moments seemed to ease the pain, salve the wound. But just as often, it loosed the pain afresh, exposed the wound again, jarred it, salted it. Gary always spoke softly. But he usually spoke with a quiet authority, a steadiness. Today, though, his voice faltered. It kept collapsing in on itself, a punctured bag that he couldn't keep the air in. The effort consumed him, and often he had to stop, to gather breath, memory, hope, just enough for a few more words.

They had no idea what to do now. They would probably have to sell the house. The prospect of trying to restart a practice was grim, for many reasons. What was God doing in all this? Had God abandoned them? Though they had guided many people through dark times—they were the friends who carried the paralyzed man to see Jesus, they were the ones who had faith for those who could find none—right now they needed someone to do that for them.

And, honestly, I felt helpless. The hope I could offer seemed no more than a greeting card, kitschy and trite, sent to someone on life support. A pat on Job's back. They needed fire; they needed steel. All I had was a hot-water bottle.

They had to be back at 12:30 for an appointment. It was twenty minutes after twelve. I was getting ready to send them away empty.

"Gary," I said, "you've done a lot of things in your life. It's not like this is all you know how to do."

"Yes, I've done many things. I have a commercial pilot's license. I was an airplane mechanic. A schoolteacher. A pastor and church planter. I ran a design and construction company. In fact, that's how I was able to support Elaine when we were first married and planting a church. Do you know that Elaine and I started the very first church in Whistler, British Columbia?"

"What years would that be?"

"1975 to, oh, '79."

"Are you talking about the little A-frame church that sat right under the gondola?"

"Yes."

"Gary," I said, "this is amazing. I went there, several times. I was a pagan. I didn't have the slightest interest in church. But I was a fanatic for skiing, and every weekend my best friend's father drove us up to Whistler on the condition that we attend the chapel service with him at the end of the day. I have to admit: I didn't listen to a word. But that would have been in 1977, right when you were there."

"Isn't that something," he said.

"You must have known the people who hosted us in their chalet that year," I said. "My friend's father set it up. It was someone involved in that church. My brother, my friend, and I stayed in someone's cabin for a weekend."

"That was probably Bill and Gloria's place. They hosted a lot of people."

"Yeah, maybe. It was quite large."

"Oh, their place wasn't too large."

"No, this was a good size. It was right next door to the cabin owned by the lady who had a yoga show on television. Karen something."

Gary and Elaine's eyes flew open.

"That was our place," they said, together.

Then a memory, clear as morning light, came to me. I saw Elaine, a young woman, a girl really, bending over to take from the oven the frozen pizza we had brought for our dinner, and then offering it to us with her wide smile. We knew we should pray, but didn't know how. So we took it to our room and ate it, graceless.

And I remembered something else: the Friday night Elaine invited us to a Bible study they were holding in their living room. We declined. We again retreated to our room. We could hear their Bible study group members arriving. Laughter and greetings. The clink of coffee cups. The soft susurrus of prayer. Then voices of varying loudness and intensity bleeding though the door of our room, slipping through the cracks like smoke. I tried to make out what they were saying, and simultaneously tried to act aloof.

I had to go to the washroom, and walked stealthily past the group. When I came out of the washroom, I didn't go straight back to the room. I hid behind the wall. To eavesdrop. I had had almost no exposure to Christians. The few I'd met seemed strange to me. Fake. Too happy. As if they shape-shifted when they saw you coming, sloughed off their ordinariness in one shake and squirmed into a polyurethane suit. But here was my opportunity: to listen secretly to how Christians spoke to one another when they didn't know anyone was listening.

A man's voice, slow, soft, measured. He was speaking encouragement to the group, telling of God's strange choreography, His hidden providence, the way He sculpted purpose out of anything, everything, nothing: failure, detour, disappointment, duty, waiting. He told how God had done this with him recently. He believed that God had called him to be a missions pilot, and so went through all the time and expense of getting his commercial pilot's license. Afterward, though, he couldn't get work anywhere—just one closed door after the next. But that led, through a series of interconnected events, to the work he did now. "I believe," the man said, "that I never would have ended up a pastor and church planter if God hadn't first opened up the door for me to be a pilot, and then shut it hard."

"Gary," I said at the lunch table, "that was you, wasn't it?"

His eyes were silvery with tears. "Yes," he said.

"Gary, I have to tell you what I did next. I went back to the room where my friend and my brother were, and I told them what I heard. I told them that Christians must be plum crazy, because they think God is personally involved in their lives. They think that God's hand is actually directing them. We all laughed at the absurdity of it.

"But Gary, I couldn't let it go. I had never heard that before. I had never even conceived of it: God cares about…me. Five years after that, I came to faith in that Christ. Today, I'm *your* pastor, Gary, Elaine, in part because of a conversation I overheard twenty-five years ago about a God who wastes nothing and who loves intimately."

It was 12:30, and they had to go. But I watched Gary and Elaine leave, and their leaving was different from their coming. They had almost crawled into that restaurant. But now a hurricane wouldn't have been able to knock them down—or me—so freshly wonder-struck were all of us by the God who meets us in the places we least suspect, at the times we need Him most.

The kingdom of heaven is like a thousand such moments, a whole lifetime of them, laid bare.

The kingdom of heaven is like a boy eavesdropping.

PART III

HEAVEN-SENT: BEING OF EARTHLY GOOD

NINE

THE ONE THING NEEDED

No one anticipated and celebrated the coming of Jesus Christ more than John the Baptist. While still curled tightly inside Elizabeth's womb, John leapt for joy at the sound of Mary's voice, somehow knowing, even in fetal darkness, whose presence he was in. Deep called to deep.

Later, as an adult, John was the first to proclaim Jesus publicly. "Behold!" he shouted from the shallows of the Jordan to the huge crowds pressing down to the river's edge. "Look, the Lamb of God, who takes away the sins of the world!" (John 1:29). Then Jesus Himself waded into that river and stood before John, asking for baptism. "But I can't," John said, amazed, afraid, thinking, *I am not worthy to untie Your shoes*. "You are the one who should baptize me." But Jesus insisted, and John obeyed.

Soon after, John's disciples worried that Jesus—*that man,* they called Him, indignant—was eclipsing John and warned him, "Rabbi, that man who was with you on the other side of the Jordan—the one you testified about—well, he is baptizing, and everyone is going to him." John replied, "He must become greater; I must become less" (John 3:26, 30).

There was a small company of saints and sages, holy men and prophets, who from the beginning recognized Jesus as *the Christ,* and with them not even one thin shadow of doubt skittered across their conviction. There were the magi, the shepherds, Isaiah, Anna, Simeon. And John.

But the greatest of these was John.

So it is all the more troubling that one day, John's faith gives out. His prickly, backwoods, scolding ways, his inability to mince words into droll euphemisms and soft hints, his political meddling devoid of statecraft, have landed him in Herod's prison. There he sits.

His thoughts are on Jesus. He isn't in prison on account of Jesus. He's there for daring to confront the powers that be. But his courage to confront those powers has everything to do with Jesus, with who he believes He is and what he believes He will do. Unlike so many others who follow Jesus, John has a heaven-borne clarity about His messianic role: It is not militaristic, but sacrificial; not imperialistic, but priestly; not a bloodstained conquest, but a blood-soaked atonement. Jesus is not the Warrior King who will remove the scourge of Rome from the earth. He is the Lamb of God, who will take away the sins of the world. John is a good theologian.

But he sits in a prison cell, listening maybe to the scrabbling of a rat in the corner, maybe to the cooing of a dove outside, maybe to the rasp and clink of an ax blade being sharpened against a whetstone in the next room. John has never sought for himself creature comforts—a cave dweller he, garbed in camel hair, nourished on wild, winged things—so the hardness and smallness and loneliness of this place fits him. But he is restless.

He is anxious.

He doubts.

The firmness in him buckles. His flinty, unflinching boldness, his clear and fierce conviction, breaks.

Surely Jesus knows my situation. He's not going to leave me here. He wouldn't. He couldn't. I've played such a crucial part in His drama. I've been there from the beginning. I'm family. And if ever Jesus had a moment to show His authority over every other principality and power, this is it.

But Jesus doesn't come. He is busy with a preaching mission in, of all places, Galilee. The backwoods. Jesus—to put it bluntly—didn't seem to care.

Is Jesus really the one?

So John sends his disciples to Jesus to ask the question: "Are you the one who was to come, or should we expect someone else?"

Jesus replies, "Go back and report to John what you hear and see: The blind receive sight, the lame walk, those who have leprosy are cured, the deaf hear, the dead are raised, and the good news is preached to the poor" (Matthew 11:3–5).

Go tell John, *You want proof that I am the one you were expecting? Look at the miracles I'm doing. Look at the people being healed and blessed.*

But then, typically, Jesus adds what seems a non sequitur: "Blessed is the man who does not fall away on account of me" (Matthew 11:6). Why would anyone fall away on account of someone who is opening the eyes of the blind, curing leprosy, making lame people walk, and preaching good news to those who never get good news? Why would anyone fall away on account of that?

Unless, of course, you're sitting in prison and, regardless of how great you've risen in the kingdom of God (see Matthew 11:11), not a single miracle is coming your way—not today, not tomorrow, not ever. And one day a man with arms like oak limbs and a hood that hides his face will stretch out your neck on a wood block, bring the burnished blade of an ax whistling down, and then serve up your head on a platter to a weak king and his spiteful wife and a foolish daughter. And Jesus will still be running His little crusade up among the yokels.

Blessed is the man who does not fall away on account of me.

One morning I got a phone call from Craig, a man who attends the church I pastor. Craig has come out of a hard past. Alcoholism. A life of petty crime. A wife who drank herself to death. And one day Craig fell off a retaining wall that he sat on while waiting for a city bus. He plummeted forty feet, shattering bone, rending muscle, rupturing insides. It broke his back. Now he's in chronic pain and unable to do any work involving sustained physical labor. He eventually got a legal settlement for his injury, but on the day he called me, the hope of that was far off. The case had suffered delay after delay, year after year, from lawyer apathy and bureaucratic backlogs.

Through it all, Craig came to Jesus Christ. He was baptized. He was freshly alive: always smiling, telling everyone about Christ, spending his days reading the Bible and Christian books, dreaming about God's plans for him now.

"Can I see you today?" Craig asked the morning he phoned.

It was a day when my wife could hardly see me. "What's up?" I asked.

"Uh…, I don't know," he said. "Don't take this too seriously…I just don't want to live anymore."

I made time. I met Craig at a coffee shop and asked him what was happening.

"It's what isn't happening," he said. "I've been waiting for a long time for something, anything, to change—my body to heal so I can work, a woman to come into my life so I'm not always alone, the court case from my accident to settle so I can get past that. But nothing ever happens. Or if it does, it just gets worse. Bad news. Another setback, and then another. I've had enough. I just would rather not have to live anymore. It's like God doesn't notice me. I don't rate His attention. I sometimes wonder if any of this Christianity stuff is even real."

Are you the one who was to come? Or should we expect someone else?

Earlier in the week I had talked with someone whose life had been utterly transformed by Christ. I spoke with another whose prayers for financial breakthrough had been answered beyond what they asked or imagined. I thought of a woman who had recently become a

Christian, who told me, "Six months ago, if someone had tried to explain to me the sheer freedom and joy I would have today, I would have thought they were nuts."

The eyes of the blind are being opened, Craig. The lame walk. The lepers are being cured. The good news, Craig—the good, stand-on-your-head, dance-in-the-streets, shout-from-the-rooftops news—is being preached to the poor.

Now how does that make you feel?

Worse.

Blessed is the man who doesn't fall away on account of the One who does all this for others, but who sometimes leaves you—*you!*—in your prison, with death just outside the door.

For me, one of the most difficult things about being a pastor is that too often I witness firsthand the lopsidedness of divine miracles.

This man over here loses his car keys and after praying finds them right there on the sofa, where he had already looked three times before. Praise the Lord! That woman over there loses her child in a park one day, snatched away when her back is turned for thirty seconds, and never sees him again.

This lady has a sinus headache, and when her friends lay hands on her, it vanishes. Isn't God good? This fellow has bone cancer and feels as if broken glass is rending his insides, but even an entire church fasting and praying for forty-eight hours doesn't relieve a single pang of his pain.

This couple sells their house two days after they list it and, in a bidding war, get $15,000 more than what they were asking, only to find the "perfect place: four thousand square feet with wood floors and three stone fireplaces on two acres with fruit trees and a duck pond" for $30,000 less than they were ready to pay. Doesn't God love to bless His children? Another couple has six children, one of them with severe learning disabilities and another with cerebral palsy, but the city inspector has just condemned their half-wide trailer, and they have no money to go elsewhere.

Blessed are those who don't fall away on account of Jesus.

Jesus often pronounced the most unlikely people blessed. The Beatitudes are our primary evidence: "Blessed are the poor...those who mourn...those who hunger and thirst...those who are persecuted" (Matthew 5:3–11). "Because you have seen me, you have believed," Jesus told Thomas after He had shown Himself, alive, to meet Thomas's demand for proof of the Resurrection. "Blessed are those who have *not seen* and yet have believed" (John 20:29, emphasis added).

What is it about the poor, the persecuted, the grieving, those who never see or touch the risen Christ, those who never taste one of His miracles—what is it about all these bruised up, broken-down, cut, and scabbed people that makes them blessed? More blessed, in fact, than the rich, the comfortable, the happy, the witnesses to resurrection?

The answer must be that those who never see, never touch, are being forced by a divine austerity, by a God who remains elusive, to grasp the substance of faith. "Faith," Hebrews says, "is being sure of what we hope for and certain of what we do not see" (Hebrews 11:1). If Jesus showed up at every funeral to raise the dead; if He showed up at every famine to multiply the meager rations into a banquet; if He showed up for every Thomas who declares, "Until I see, until I touch, I won't believe"; if He showed up in every prison cell to fling the iron bars wide and, by angel-escort, waltz the prisoner out—well, indeed, our faith would be strengthened.

But also weakened. Faith would more and more twine its roots just beneath the surface, splaying wide but not striking deep, gathering its nourishment from the capriciousness of circumstances. Jesus calls miracles *signs*. The writer of Hebrews calls them *shadows*. Miracles are meant to point to something bigger, more real, more alive, than themselves. But when faith comes to depend on miracle, it ends up mistaking the sign for the destination, the shadow for the substance, the nourishment for the soil itself.

Miracles, for all their power to shore up faith, are themselves rickety things, flimsy, vaporous. They can only point, mutely, to the place we need to go. They can only cast, coolly, the flat dark shape, devoid of detail, of the thing we need to embrace. At best, they are silhouettes, showing us in outline, without color or feature, the reality we need to behold. They are the fingerprints of God, a clue to His presence, but they are not His hand.

Blessed are those who don't need the sign, the shadow. Blessed are those who, bereft of the miraculous cure or rescue or windfall or breakthrough, believe anyhow, turn and embrace the Reality anyhow. They have not fallen away *on account of Jesus*. They have grasped that a relationship with Jesus is different from a bargain or a contract with Him—an "if You do this for me, I will do this for You" arrangement. They have understood that a miracle is as much a veil as a shrine, that it conceals God as much as it discloses Him, that it can become not the "sign" that points to God, but the diversion that keeps us from Him.[21] They have refused to stand in the company of those who "demand a sign," whose demand is not an expression of their faith, but a display of their "wicked and adulterous" hearts (Matthew 12:39). They are, rather, among the pure in heart who will see God— the Reality who casts the shadow, the Destination to whom the signs point.

Hoping *for something* is very different from hoping *in Someone*. This is what I told Craig that day. The difference is not one of degree, but of kind: To *hope in* Jesus is categorically different than to *hope for* anything He might do for me or for others.

Hope that is built on Jesus' feats and wonderworks—even if He were to perform such things over and over on demand—is hope built on sand. "Many will say to me on that day, 'Lord, Lord, did we not prophesy in your name, and in your name drive out demons and perform many miracles?' Then I will tell them plainly, 'I never knew you. Away from me, you evildoers!'" (Matthew 7:22–23).

I do hope that Jesus will do some things—reverse my male pattern baldness or give me fresh insights for the book I'm writing or protect my wife as she drives to town this morning or help Craig find a wife and a job. I hope for some of these things with more earnestness and ache than others, but my faith does not rest in them. They are in some ways the sentiments of faith, the feelings and wishes that arise from having faith, but they are not what grounds or gives rise to my faith. As the old hymn says, "My hope is built on nothing less than Jesus' blood and righteousness."

"If only for this life we have hope in Christ," the apostle Paul wrote, "we are to be pitied more than all men" (1 Corinthians 15:19). We can hope *in Christ,* but if that hope is only for the here and the now, if it is strictly earth-bound, we are in the deepest sense *hopeless.* If the fullness of our hope is no more than a divine miracle brokered in the temporal realm—our sicknesses cured, our ruptured relationships mended, the prisoners set free, the famished fed—our lives are ultimately pathetic, pitiful. Because hope then is only hope *for something* I might get, not hope *in Someone* I know. The apostle John illustrates this truth in a key Gospel event, the feeding of the crowd.

Five thousand people followed Jesus out into the wilderness, and in His compassion He taught them. But it got late, and they were hungry and far from their homes. So Jesus multiplied loaves and fishes to feed them. Then Jesus departed, but the people followed Him again. They came to His church because He met their earthly needs: He gave them bread and broiled fish when they were hungry, and compassionate sermons—perhaps on how to cope with stress and anxiety—when they were confused and disoriented. He gave them hope for this life.

So they came again, and Jesus taught them again, but the next time was different. This time His sermon frightened away all but the sternest and sturdiest of them:

> "I tell you the truth, you are looking for me, not because you saw miraculous signs but because you ate the loaves and had your fill. Do not work for food that spoils, but for food that endures to eternal life, which the Son of Man will give you.
> "I am the bread of life.
> "If anyone eats of this bread, he will live forever."
> (John 6:26–27, 35, 51)

Almost everyone left, hungry, grumbling, embittered. "This is a hard teaching," they complained. "Who can accept it?" (v. 60).

Jesus was magnificently aloof about their leaving. He came to seek and save the lost and to doctor the sick, but He never chases anyone. He only and always gives a stark choice—it's this or that; it's yes or no—and a heartbeat to decide. At that moment He turned even to His disciples and threw down the gauntlet: "You do not want to leave too, do you?" He asked (v. 67).

"Lord, to whom shall we go?" Peter responded. "You have the words of eternal life. We believe and know that you are the Holy One of God" (vv. 68–69).

Ah, Peter. Big-boned and half-cocked Peter, more brash than wise, more rash than daring. He gabbles when even the angels are silent and is mute when even the stones cry out. He is a bully and a coward and a braggart, but just when you want to be done with him, to dismiss him as a fool, he does something of such utter pure-heartedness and unspeakable wisdom that your anger and suspicion toward him melt away, and you remember why you've always liked him.

"But what about you?" Jesus once asked him. "Who do you say I am?" And Peter answered, "You are the Christ, the Son of the living God," to which Jesus replied, "Blessed are you, Simon son of Jonah" (Matthew 16:15–17).

This is a moment like that one. "Do you want to leave?" Jesus asked.

To whom shall we go? You have the words of eternal life. We believe and know that You are the Holy One of God.

If only for this life we have hope in Christ, we're to be pitied more than all men.

We hope in Christ not just because He feeds us, or heals us, or routs our enemies. Indeed, sometimes he doesn't do any of that; sometimes He turns us away empty-bellied, cancer-ridden, defeated. No, we hope in Christ because of who He is, because *He has the words of eternal life,* and because anyone "who feeds on this bread will live forever." Because the world—and all its bread and all its fish and all its jewels and all its wonders and all its everything—is not enough. Life doesn't justify living.

Only eternity does. And Jesus alone grants that.

But here John is in prison. The stone walls press close, taunting. The stifling, rancid air goes down his throat like a burr, catching, stinging.

His voice, thin and dry, sounds far away: a voice, crying, in the wilderness. He instructs his disciples: "Go ask Jesus, 'Are you the one who was to come?'" He pauses. Some gray shadow of memory crosses his face. "'Or should we expect someone else?'" (see Matthew 11:3).

They leave. He waits. The waiting is terrible. A waiting like that is an unfortified city, begging for vandals, plunderers, ghosts. John tries to sleep, but he is too anxious and too weary for it. So he waits. His disciples return and report all that they have seen and heard.

"There was this old woman, John, bent and twisted as that lone tree in the potter's field, and Jesus spoke a word and she straightened up, supple as a willow branch, and started dancing. And this man, his eyes were dead as stones, and Jesus spit on His fingers and rubbed them, and when the man opened his eyes, they shone like wet jewels. He laughed; he started singing. And that leper…and those beggars…and even a dead child—John, we saw it with our own eyes—Jesus brought that little girl back to life. The parents—oh, John, I've never seen joy like that.

"Oh, and John, Jesus said something strange just before we left. It was a word, He said, just for you: 'Blessed is he who does not fall away on account of Me.'"

John, I think, smiled. And he knew: Jesus *is* the one.

TEN

A TOUR OF THE LOWER GALLERIES

The Christian life comes down to one thing: faith. We are saved by faith, not by works. Anything done without faith is sin. The apostle Paul sums it up in one elegant phrase: "We live by faith, not by sight" (2 Corinthians 5:7). True life—eternal, abundant, holy life—is not by works or by sight. It's only by faith. We don't just pray by faith, or give by faith, or go on mission trips by faith. We live by faith.

In one sense this is obvious. We have no other option. Just getting up in the morning requires an enormous act of faith. The food you blithely eat—even after you've seen all those science documentaries about how each bite writhes and crawls with a zillion hairy, spiny, scaly, leggy little creatures—you eat by faith. The car you drive—despite all the thousand sundry things that can go awry: brackets sheering, gas tanks exploding, lug nuts threading loose, coronary attack victims or reckless drunks careening toward you—you drive by faith. Many of us have built our houses atop the slippery joints of massive earth plates. We live astride the crack of doom. But happily, merrily, we shop and jog and go to meetings and frolic at playgrounds and lay our heads down at night beneath thin plaster ceilings—all with no perceptible speeding up of our pulses. We live by faith all day and all night long.

But the stakes are actually much higher: "Without faith it is impossible to please God" (Hebrews 11:6). Faith is more than what we live by. It is the medium through which we know and are known by God.

Imagine that you just found out you have a rare and terminal illness. You sit down with your doctor.

"Is there no hope?" you ask.

"Well," he says, "there is one thing. Without this one thing, it's over. But with this one thing, you will be completely healed. But let me be utterly clear: It's impossible for you to live without this one thing."

What would you say?

"Listen, Doc, you're boring me. My favorite sitcom is starting in five minutes, and I wouldn't miss it for anything. I don't have time for these silly cat-and-mouse games. See ya."

Or, "Well…that's interesting. But, Doctor, that's *your* opinion. You are completely entitled to it, and I'm sure it makes you feel better for having expressed it. But I resent your attempt to impose it upon me.

I really don't need this kind of psychological blackmail, this medical fascism. Good-bye and good riddance."

Or, "What? What is it? Tell me now! I have to know, and I won't leave until I do!"

Of course, the only sane response is the last one.

If we are *saved* by faith, and if we *live* by faith, and if it is *impossible* to please God without faith, the only sane response is: *What is it? What is this faith? You have to tell me! I have to know, and I'm not leaving until I do!*

Faith is not sticky sentiment or dry academics. It's not an emergency provision for the times we're unable to compile enough hard, cold facts or weave a tight enough web of logic to explain things. It's not the last-ditch stand beyond biology, physics, psychology. It's not something we muster—a rough mix of sentimentality, piety, nostalgia, and stubbornness—only for the hard times and the dark times. It is more than a flutter in the belly or a warm glow in the heart, more than nodding approval to a set of doctrinal statements. Faith is sinewy and feisty and vigorous, a living hope and a deep certainty that sparks life into all we are and all we do.

"Faith is being sure of what we hope for and certain of what we do not see" (Hebrews 11:1). It's being sure and certain. As the writer of Hebrews unfolds this claim—not in some philosophical and pedantic way, but with example after example of what such faith looks and feels and sounds like in living, breathing human beings—it becomes obvious that faith *is* something and that faith *does* something.

By faith, we *understand that the invisible preceded the visible.*
By faith, Abel *made his offerings to God.*
By faith, Elijah *didn't taste death.*
By faith, Noah *trusted in God,* even when told to build an ark in a desert.
By faith, Abraham *was willing to risk and to sacrifice.*
By faith, Isaac *blessed his children.*
By faith, Joseph *died well.*
By faith, Moses' parents *were unafraid of earthly powers.*
By faith, Moses *chose to suffer for the kingdom of God.*
By faith, the Israelites *crossed the Red Sea.*
By faith, Joshua *saw Jericho's walls come down.*
By faith, Rahab *staked everything on God's kingdom to come.*
By faith, others *triumphed over huge odds or endured when triumphed over.*

Charles Spurgeon once told his congregation about a trip he had taken to the Palace of Versailles in France. The upper galleries in the palace were stocked with famous paintings by famous painters of famous people, each of them in frozen portrait, mute and motionless for all time. Spurgeon noticed that visitors paused to look at the first two or three of these portraits, but then lost interest and passed by the rest with hardly a first glance, let alone a second.

Downstairs, though, in the lower galleries, the visitors' flagging interest suddenly revived. There, many of the paintings depicted people *doing* things: fighting wars, making speeches, galloping on horses, sailing in storms.

Spurgeon:

> Not the people but their actions engross attention. Portraits have no charm when scenes of stirring interest are set in rivalry with them.... If we would impress we must act. The dignity of standing still will never win the prize; we must run for it.[22]

Hebrews 11 takes us on a tour of the lower galleries and shows us men and women living by faith. Not one of them *sits* for a portrait. They choose and bless, risk and trust, give and suffer. They pursue and they forsake. They are willing to face death by faith, and because of faith, they don't taste death.

The tour concludes with an exhortation: "Since we are surrounded by such a great cloud of witnesses, let us throw off everything that hinders and the sin that so easily entangles, and let us *run with perseverance the race marked out for us*" (Hebrews 12:1, emphasis added).

The dignity of standing still will never win the prize; we must run for it.

Faith calls us to action. We're surrounded by the portraits. These are not a clutch of docile saints, pinch-faced and stiffly poised, their arms and hands neatly folded like banquet napkins across their laps.

They did more than just observe life and comment on it; they lived their lives to the full. Their actions were prompted by the sure conviction that God is God and that what matters most is what He thinks and does and invites us to do. They knew whom they believed and were confident that He was able to keep that which they had entrusted to Him.

So they ran. They finished the race. They fought the good fight. They kept the faith. They were of much earthly good.

Now it's your turn.

So faith is and faith acts. But faith also has an object. The action of faith is rooted in an assurance of *something*. The key phrases in the definition of faith in Hebrews are these: "being sure of *what we hope for*...being certain *of what we do not see*" (11:1, emphasis added). The crucial question, then, is simply: "What is this unseen thing that we hope for?"

What do you hope for? Have you ever gotten what you hoped for? Oh yes—you hoped for that Rocky Mountain twenty-eight-speed bike, and you got it. Even in the color you wanted: blue.

But was it really what you hoped for? There are two remarkable lines in Hebrews 11: "All these people were still living by faith when they died. They did not receive the things promised. These were all commended for their faith, yet none of them received what had been promised" (vv. 13, 39). Some of them suffered grotesquely. Their lives were a chronicle of gothic terror. Others accomplished stupendous feats and witnessed staggering miracles. Their lives were a pageantry of daring and triumph. But in their lifetimes, none of them received what they hoped for.

What were they hoping for?

Ready?

Heaven.

You saw that coming all along.

Faith is nothing if there is nothing beyond earth. It is nothing if this world is enough. Ultimately, faith is hope in the city that Jesus' blood secured for us, that He is preparing for us, and where He is now seated at the right hand of God awaiting us—the place where on *that day* and on all days after we will see Him face-to-face. Faith without deeds is dead, but faith without heaven is dead too.

We live by faith because faith is living. It works in us the same way blood does, by moving through every part, animating the whole. But if we fail to live in certain hope of what God has promised, our faith withers. We get afraid and cling to our lives or our stuff. We sit still and prim for our portrait, or we entangle in sin. Either way, paralyzed or entangled, we don't run. We're of little earthly good. We tiptoe well-worn paths and backtrack at the first rustling in the bushes. We hug the shore and scuttle back panic-stricken at the first sign of a real wind. We try to save our life, and lose it. Losing faith affects our spiritual life the same way a heart seizure affects our physical life: It strikes us down body and soul, and if not reversed, it kills us.

The apostle Paul insisted that hope in Jesus Christ must incorporate hope in the resurrection—that it must encompass and be centered on a hope beyond this life. He states it flatly: "If only for this life we have hope in Christ, we are to be pitied more than all men" (1 Corinthians 15:19). A relationship with Jesus Christ that *is only for this life* is pitiful—more pitiful than promiscuity, drug addiction, wasting illness, relentless suffering.

"If the dead are not raised," Paul says, "let us eat and drink, for tomorrow we die" (1 Corinthians 15:32). If there is no heaven, live for your appetites. Make your stomach your god. Get what you can while you can. Why not? Why deny yourself? Why take up a cross and follow Jesus? Why give your hard-won money to church and charity? Why volunteer your precious time to help others? Why do anything—tolerate any inconvenience, endure any trial, take any risk—if there's not something in it for you right here and now? Why be of any earthly good? Tomorrow you die.

That's *if* the dead are not raised. But what if they are? What if God does reward those who earnestly seek Him? What if God's ultimate promise and prize is that you will be transformed and live with Him forever?

How do we know which claim to believe?

There is ultimately only one way. Through faith. By being certain of Things Unseen.

Through faith we become certain of heaven. It becomes as sure as the ground beneath our feet. No, more so. Heaven, Hebrews 12 concludes, is the one thing that remains after everything else—sea and sky, earth and air, tree and stone—shakes to dust, burns to ashes, scatters to oblivion. There is a kingdom that cannot be shaken, and those who live by faith receive it.

Since we're receiving such a kingdom, what kind of people should we be? The answer is almost circular: We're to be people who live by faith. And that means that sometimes we'll do things that, judged by earthly standards, make no sense. John says that since we live in the hope that when Christ appears, we shall be made like Him, we ought to purify ourselves (see 1 John 3:3). Peter says that since everything around us will one day be destroyed, we ought to live holy and godly lives (see 2 Peter 3:11).

Purity. Holiness. Godliness. This is life against the grain. It requires nimble, shrewd resistance to the world's varied wooings and tauntings, its seductiveness and vindictiveness. Who is equal to such a task? Only those who believe deeply that Christ will appear and make them like Him. Only those who believe firmly that a kingdom is coming that cannot be shaken, while all else will be destroyed. Only those who stake everything on that belief. Faith makes them certain of what they do not see.

All those who have such hope live this way. They're of much earthly good.

Stay in the race. That's how Hebrews concludes its tour of portraits in the lower gallery, its survey of those who lived by faith: "Therefore, since we are surrounded by such a great cloud of witnesses, let us throw off everything that hinders and the sin that so easily entangles, and let us run with perseverance the race marked out for us" (Hebrews 12:1).

Don't lose heart, because all these people—Abel, Noah, Abraham, Moses, Rahab…all of them—press in now to watch you run your race. Up there is Abraham. Over there…look! It's Moses, with his mother, his father, his sister. And across from them…hello! It's Isaac, and Jacob, and Joseph…and isn't that Gideon with them? With such a great cloud of witnesses gathered to cheer us on, who would flag, dally, turn back? What else is there to do except finish the race?

Whenever I read this passage, I think of Rick Hanson, the paraplegic athlete who from 1985 to 1987 circled the globe on his wheelchair to raise awareness of and money for spinal cord research.

It was a grueling trip. There are photos of Rick in all kinds of weather: burning heat, the air hazy with dust; choking humidity, the air puckering with moisture; slashing rain; swirling blizzard; howling wind. There are photos of him in all terrain: desert wastelands, dense forests, patchwork farmlands, golden savannas, craggy mountains. He twists his head downward as he pushes himself through a vast barrenness of prairie, the land opaque with winter cold, one lonely narrow road stretching straight and gray forever. He strains his head back, his neck fluted with stretched cords, his arms taut with aching muscles, his body a skein of bulging veins and his fists like stones, as he climbs the near impossible steepness of China's Great Wall. He thrusts his head forward, flintlike, his jaw set firm, as he wheels through the rain-blackened street of some nondescript city, its inhabitants indifferent to his plight and his cause.

Mile upon mile upon tiresome mile. Hands thick with calluses. Thighs bruised, back blistered. Weariness in him like a rumor of death.

But on May 23, 1987, Rick Hanson came home.

When he was still far away, many miles from Vancouver, people gathered to welcome him. As he got nearer, the crowd thickened along both sides of the highway: hundreds of people, then thousands, then thousands on thousands. They roared, clapped, cheered, wept. They threw flowers. Rick moved with power and grace, effortless. He climbed Thermal Drive in Coquitlam, one snaking precipitous section steeper than the steepest part of the Great Wall of China, and did it with jaunty ease.

And then he headed toward B.C. Place. A capacity crowd of sixty thousand people—national and international dignitaries, rock stars and movie stars, television crews, family, friends, those lucky enough to get tickets—waited inside, delirious with anticipation. As Rick got nearer the stadium, the streets grew impossibly dense with people. Helicopters hovered overhead. Police in cars and on motorcycles flanked his sides. Other wheelchair athletes joined him, coming up behind like a legion of charioteers, flashes from their spinning spokes spilling down the roadway like fistfuls of tossed coins.

As Rick came over the Cambie Street Bridge, he could hear, even above the din of the crowd around him, the roar of voices coming from inside the stadium. A hurricane brewing. A landslide loosening. But not even that prepared him for what happened next.

Rick Hanson entered B.C. Place. He swooped through the wide lower gates and glided out onto the stadium floor—and sixty thousand people went berserk. Leaping, dancing, blowing horns, whirling clackers, the air shrill with wolf whistles, exploding with applause, swelling with throaty shouts of welcome and triumph. Wild, raucous, hypnotic. Metal girders hummed like struck tuning forks from all the noise burned into them. A roar to deafen, to open the ears of the deaf, to raise the dead. And every time it seemed about to taper off, a fresh wind caught it and carried it higher, louder, brighter, fuller.

Such a great cloud of witnesses.

A great cloud of witnesses cheering us on too, cheering us all the way home.

But that's not all. That's not even the best.

There's the prize. It's the prize for which Jesus calls us heavenward, and it is more than a crown, more than a medal, more than a trophy, more than a kiss from a pretty, svelte girl.

The prize is the Lord Himself. "Let us fix our eyes on Jesus, the author and perfecter of our faith." The faith we've been talking about does not come from within us; it's not some conviction dredged up by dint of will. It is created, bestowed, and perfected by Another. Fix your eyes on Jesus, "who for the joy set before him endured the cross, scorning its shame, and sat down at the right hand of the throne of God. Consider him who endured such opposition from sinful men, so that you will not grow weary and lose heart" (Hebrews 12:2–3).

Consider Him. Fix your eyes on Him. He's the reason you've been called heavenward. The One you see now only from a distance, sketchy, whose voice you hear now only from far away, staccato, on *that day* you will see and hear with undiminished clarity. He waits to give Himself to you and to use all the power He possesses—the power by which he rules planets and commands angels—to transform you so that you are just like Him.

> Our citizenship is in heaven. And we eagerly await a Savior from there, the Lord Jesus Christ, who, by the power that enables him to bring everything under his control, will transform our lowly bodies so that they will be like his glorious body. (Philippians 3:20–21)

You're heaven-bent. You eagerly await a Savior who, in turn, eagerly awaits you. There's a huge company with you, cheering every move you and your Savior make closer to each other. His reward isn't in His hands. The marks of it, the price He paid to win it: those are in His hands, both hands, indelible. But the reward is in Him. The reward is Him.

He pours out grace for you to finish the race. He pours out more grace when you stumble, grow weary, fall down, lose heart. He stands at the head of the course and, while all the saints who have gone before line the roadway and cheer riotously, He stretches out His arms wide in exuberant welcome, exultant congratulation.

I'm telling you: Keep your eyes on the prize and finish this race.

The Spanish philosopher Miguel de Unamuno sought to fashion a religion he deemed intellectually respectable. He wanted it shorn clean of what he considered medieval superstitions, fumigated of any whiff of divine wrath and rewards, purged of all hints of an afterlife. But he thought he'd better test his idea among the nonintellectual class.

He found a rather simple-minded peasant and asked him what he thought of a religion that posited faith in God, but not fear of hell, not hope of heaven.

The peasant thought a moment. Then he asked—I can see the great cloud of witnesses cheering him on—"So what is this God for?"[23]

ELEVEN

LOOK UP

P aul frustrates me sometimes. The apostle Paul, that is. He com-
bines an odd mix of qualities: blunt as a hurled stone, searing
as a branding iron, cryptic as a hieroglyph, didactic as a school-
marm. At times he seems timid, at other times dauntless. He often says
two different things—yes, no—and holds to both without compro-
mise. One minute he's preaching hard against legalism, toppling the
Babel-tower of rules like Samson tearing down the Philistines' temple.
The next, he's a backwoods Bible-thumper sternly warning, thickly
scowling, every word sharp with the smell of brimstone burning.

"You're free people," he declares. "Stop submitting to this endless
litany of do's and don'ts. Where has that ever got anybody?" Then, just
when we're about to heed him, he turns back: "Oh, and remember:
you must, you can't, you always, you never…"

It's frustrating.

Like in Colossians:

Since you died with Christ to the basic principles of this world, why, as though you still belonged to it, do you submit to its rules: "Do not handle! Do not taste! Do not touch!"? These are all destined to perish with use, because they are based on human commands and teachings. Such regulations indeed have an appearance of wisdom, with their self-imposed worship, their false humility and their harsh treatment of the body, but they lack any value in restraining sensual indulgence. (2:20–23)

A more thorough dismantling of legalism could hardly be imagined. In a few tightly argued and crisply rendered sentences, Paul deals with the flaw at the heart of a rule-making, rule-keeping religion. The rules, for one, are too often man-made, a rickety moral code cobbled together out of our anxiety and pride. But that's not the worst of it. This is: The rules are useless. *They lack any value in restraining sensual indulgence.* They can no more quiet the beast or rouse the sloth within us than a paper wall can hold back fire.

In fact, Paul elsewhere argues that rules do the opposite: Far from nurturing glad obedience, they actually prompt us to temptation and rebellion. This is true even when the rules are divine in origin. "I would not have known what coveting really was if the law had not said, 'Do not covet.' But sin, seizing the opportunity afforded by the

commandment, produced in me every kind of covetous desire"
(Romans 7:7–8).

I know exactly how this works. Tell me "You can't," and I ache to
defy you. *Just watch me,* I say to myself. Tell me "You must," and some
coil of stubbornness tightens and hardens inside me. *Try to make me,*
I think. Sometimes my wife leans over to me in a public place and
whispers, "Don't look now, but there's a man behind you in a bur-
gundy sweater, and I think it's Melissa's second cousin." *Don't look
now.* I may have no interest whatsoever in Melissa's second cousin—I
may not even remember who Melissa is, exactly—but some temptation to turn and *look now* seizes me. That temptation springs up as
thick and swift as Jack's beanstalk from the tiny seed of those three
little words: *Don't look now.* A moment before, I had not the slightest
itch to look anywhere, at anybody, at any time. It had never entered
my head. *But sin, seizing the opportunity afforded by the commandment,
produced in me every kind of covetous desire.*

Such is legalism. Plain and simple, it never makes us holy. It
works, in fact, in the other direction, enticing us to be outlaws.

So Paul obliterates it. He tears it down and sets it burning with his
own bare hands. Then he stands over the razed and smoking ruins,
knocking the dust off himself, pleased at a job well done. And just
when we think he's finished and we can all go home dancing, he clears
his throat and speaks:

Put to death, therefore, whatever belongs to your earthly
nature: sexual immorality, impurity, lust, evil desires and

greed, which is idolatry. Because of these, the wrath of God is coming. You used to walk in these ways, in the life you once lived. But now you must rid yourselves of all such things as these: anger, rage, malice, slander, and filthy language from your lips. Do not lie to each other. (Colossians 3:5–9)

Don't live like you used to. Don't give in to all those old conceits and deceits, those habitual cravings and ancient appetites. Kill that stuff. Get rid of it. God hates it, and you don't want to be found with it around the house when God comes to visit.

Don't submit to rules.

Live by the rules.

Well, Paul, which is it?

But Paul has a secret. He utters it so quickly that we almost miss it. It's the secret of how we can be both free and holy—free without rule-breaking, holy without rule-keeping.

Paul's secret is heavenly-mindedness. In between dismantling the tower of legalism and building ramparts against the onslaught of license, he says this:

Since, then, you have been raised with Christ, set your hearts on things above, where Christ is seated at the right hand of God. Set your minds on things above, not on earthly things. For you died, and your life is now hidden with Christ in God.

When Christ, who is your life, appears, then you also will appear with him in glory. (Colossians 3:1–4)

God intends the holy life be an odyssey of wonder. The religious impulse tends to make it into a journey both dreary and heavy, perilous and plodding. But God designed holiness to be invigorating, the discovery of life so abundant that if He didn't unveil it for us, we would forever lack the imagination even to ask for it.

Jesus one day stops at Matthew's tax-collecting booth. The taxman grubs and mumbles, stacks coins, scribbles knotlike numbers on parchment. A criminal bureaucrat, that one. He lives a life of racketeering and ledger-keeping all bound up together. "Come, follow Me," Jesus says. Matthew looks up, startled. *What kind of greeting is this?* One thing it's not: an invitation to carry on life as he's always known it. No, this is a dare and a promise, a call to the holy wild.

"Matthew," Jesus seems to say, "is this the life you want, this stealing and hoarding, making enemies for all the wrong reasons? This rule-keeping and rule-breaking all at once? Matthew, don't you ever dream? Don't you hope you wake before you die? Come, follow Me. I will make you rich in things that neither rule-breaking nor rule-keeping can ever give you. I will make you free and I will make you holy."

Free and holy.

But if we're to see it that way—and live into it—it will be because we have learned to set our hearts and minds on things above. Apart from that, holiness is austere and cumbersome, a stone on our back, a fetter on our leg. Without a larger hope, we sour and grow weary, and the temptation is just to throw it all off and run amok. But when we become heavenly-minded, we sprout wings. We learn a whole new way of being.

Set your heart on things above. Set your mind on things above. Fix your eyes not on what is seen, but on what is unseen. These are simple disciplines that change everything. They are small shifts in focus and perspective that usher in a vast world of wonders—a world where we are free and holy, where we are free to be holy.

The Liberator has come. Jesus Christ, Lord of creation and redemption, gathered all His enemies in one nail-driven hand and routed them. Then He made a spectacle of them. He shackled them and dragged them bruised and stumbling behind cartloads of plunder taken from their own tents (see 2 Corinthians 2:14; Colossians 2:15).

And we're free.

A friend of mine, a key church leader in Canada, told me that in second grade he was the teacher's pet. He relished that. He hovered near the teacher, dutiful and attentive, ready at her subtlest cue to do her bidding. One day, about halfway through the year, she sent him to the staff room to fetch something, and while there, he accidentally knocked a ceramic teapot onto the floor. It shattered. His teacher walked in and saw it. Her face sharpened and closed with anger. "You big stupid oaf," she said. "How could you be so clumsy?"

His world fell apart. He spent the rest of his school year trying harder and harder to prove her wrong. But everything he did, or failed to do, only seemed to confirm her verdict. So he gave up, gave in. He couldn't keep the rules, so he decided to break them. If he couldn't wear the name *teacher's pet,* he'd wear his new name: *big, stupid, clumsy oaf.*

Over the next several years, he went from a model student to a problem child. His grades slid. He rabble-roused and back-talked. He spent a lot of time either out in the hallway or down at the principal's office. He got involved with the wrong people, doing the wrong things.

Captive.

Then, in college, he came to Jesus Christ, and discovered freedom. Jesus triumphed over the keeping of the rules and the breaking of the rules. He triumphed over the harrowing silence when my friend waited for a word of solace, over the withering curse when he longed for benediction. He triumphed over the need to prove anyone wrong and over the despair that drove him to prove them right. He triumphed over all the names that had been laid upon him in anger or fear or bitterness. He triumphed over all the words and deeds that first scored him like wounds, and then branded him like birthmarks. He triumphed over the sin that caused these things and the sin that bred in the soil of them.[24]

But my friend also discovered that it takes discipline of heart and mind to live into that freedom—as he puts it, to let "the Master's story define your own story." It took Israel a long time and many lessons after they had escaped slavery in Egypt to behave and think as free people—if ever they did. It takes a prisoner, once released, many seasons to break out of the deeper confinement of habit and attitude.

"Once you were alienated from God and were enemies *in your minds* because of your evil behavior," Paul says. "But now he has reconciled you by Christ's physical body through death to present you holy in his sight, without blemish and free from accusation" (Colossians 1:21–22, emphasis added). Once we were far away from God, His enemies, *in our minds*. That enmity and estrangement manifests itself as "evil behavior." But its power to hold us is in our minds.

Alienation from God is not just about how we act. It's about how we think. It's *in our minds*. This means that the key to understanding our freedom in Christ—that we are no longer alienated from God, but are now reconciled to Him through Christ and have been made holy in His sight, without blemish or accusation—*is also in our minds*. Make no mistake: Christ's redemptive work is a reality that happened *out there,* in place and time. His reconciling us to God, His presenting us holy and unblemished before God, is a reality, independent of whether we understand it fully or not. *But its power to change us is in our minds.* We are transformed through the renewing of our minds, and only then are we able to test and approve God's good, perfect, and pleasing will (see Romans 12:2).

So freedom and holiness come through what we set our minds on. "We demolish arguments and every pretension that sets itself up against the knowledge of God," Paul says in another place, "and we take captive every thought to make it obedient to Christ" (2 Corinthians 10:5). The word in Greek for *take captive* literally means *to take prisoner.* We take prisoner, he says, anything that tries to take us prisoner. Thoughts, accusations, false affections, deceits—anything that tries to eclipse the reality of God's work—we round that up, lock that up, beat that down, throw that out. And we can, because Jesus has already triumphed over all of it.

Who hurt you? What haunts you? What shame weighs on you? What scars mark you?

"You big, stupid, clumsy oaf."

What did you just call me? Get in the cage and shut up. The Lord who holds all things together has broken your power and given me a new name. And He has given me authority over you. So you're under arrest.

Listen again to Paul's secret of the holy life: "Since, then, you have been raised with Christ, set your hearts on things above, where Christ is seated at the right hand of God. Set your minds on things above, not on earthly things" (Colossians 3:1–2).

Look up. That's the discipline. Simply look up. Make things above your obsession. Become fiercely heavenly-minded, spiritually-minded, Christ-minded.

That is our best hope of growing in both freedom and holiness. The degree to which we do not set our heart and mind on things above is the degree to which we will stall and grow bitter, become bored or afraid *down here*. Without a magnificent obsession, holiness is not a garden, but a tundra: an austere land of weariness and drivenness, heartache and hard-heartedness, loopholes and rules. Without looking up, we're of little earthly good, and we find little good on earth.

But take heart. Christ has overcome the world, and thus freed us to live in it with joy and vigor. Look up and see Him, reigning and interceding, and do not grow weary or lose heart. Fix your eyes on Jesus. Paradoxically, the things of earth will grow not only strangely dim in that light, but strangely beautiful too.

"Take hold," Paul tells Timothy, "of the eternal life to which you were called when you made your good confession in the presence of many witnesses" (1 Timothy 6:12). Meaning: Live in light of forever. Choose and think and act now in the light, not of what was, not of what is, but of what is to come.

Our future—who we are becoming, where we are going—matters more than our past—where and who we have been. Our future has more power to name us and define us than our past. Consummation swallows origins. Destiny, not history, is the ultimate ground of our identity. How does a prostitute named Rahab, a Moabite outsider named Ruth, an incestuous schemer named Tamar, an adulteress named Bathsheba, end up in the birth line of Jesus? Because in God's economy the person we become, not the person we have been, is the person we truly are.

Jesus had a habit that would make Him a poor recruitment officer in a modern business: He never asked people about their past. He never demanded a résumé. He never conducted carefully scripted interviews with discipleship candidates, probing for skills and experiences that qualified them for the work, for traits and mistakes that might have disqualified them, never ran them through a battery of psychological tests and attitudinal questionnaires. "Well, Peter, according to Myers-Briggs, you're an ESTP, which means…" "John, the LPT14 instrument reveals that you…"

The Pharisees never tired of complaining that Jesus failed to do background checks on people. *Look, He eats with sinners. If this man were truly a prophet,* Simon the Pharisee thinks on one occasion, *He would know who this woman is who is touching Him* (see Luke 7:36–39).

Jesus' typical recruitment interview went like this: "Come, follow Me."

Say no, and remain who you've been. Once a tax collector, always a tax collector.

Say yes, and hang on for the ride. The glory that is to be revealed begins to shape you in ways your past cannot control.

And we…are being transformed into his likeness with ever-increasing glory. (2 Corinthians 3:18)

Our citizenship is in heaven. And we eagerly await a Savior from there, the Lord Jesus Christ, who, by the power that enables him to bring everything under his control, will transform our lowly bodies so that they will be like his glorious body. (Philippians 3:20–21)

Dear friends, now we are children of God, and what we will be has not yet been made known. But we know that when he appears, we shall be like him. (1 John 3:2)

All this is hard, almost impossible, to grasp. Imagine trying to explain to a caterpillar—even a smart one—what it will be one day. There it is, fuzzy and many-legged, curling and scuttling along branch or ground. Blind, earth-bound, wormlike. "One day," you explain, "you're going to wrap up in this thick, sticky band of threads and hang from a twig. And then, after a while, you will emerge. You will be utterly transformed. You will no longer crawl. You will have eyes, and you will see. You will have wings, delicate pinions sculpted and painted more exquisitely than any artwork man's hands have ever rendered, more beautiful than lace and paper and watercolor. You will fly. No, more: You will dance on air."[25]

If you could convince the caterpillar this was so, what huge incentive it might have as it labored along in its hunching, shuffling, blind-eyed belly crawl.

"When Christ, who is your life, appears," Paul says, "then you also will appear with him in glory" (Colossians 3:4). Who you will one day be in Christ is more than you could ever ask or imagine. When He appears, the real you will break forth in all your dazzling wonder and splendor.

The best is yet to come.

Several years ago, a millionaire named Eugene Lang spoke to a class of sixth graders at a school in New York's East Harlem. This was an inner-city school. The building was ramshackle; the morale even more so. The statistics gave a dismal picture: Within three years, most of the students would drop out to join gangs, sell drugs, turn tricks. Many would end up in prison. Many would be dead before the age of twenty. If history were destiny, most of these sixth-grade students wouldn't get a break and didn't stand a chance.

Eugene Lang looked at them, and his heart broke. He put down his notes. "Stay in school," he pleaded. "Stay in school, and I will pay the college tuition for every one of you."

Nearly 90 percent of that class graduated and went on to college. One boy described it this way: "I had something to look forward to, something waiting for me. It was a golden feeling."[26]

If Paul were here, he'd say something like this: "Stay the course. Stay in Christ's school of freedom and holiness. Stay, because not only has He already paid the tuition, but you can hardly imagine what graduation looks like—the glory that will be revealed."

Set your hearts on things above. Set your minds on things above.

Look up.

Twelve

DEAD ALREADY

There is a surprising, ironic reason for looking up: We're dead already. "Set your minds on things above..." Paul instructs. *"For you died,* and your life is now hidden with Christ in God" (Colossians 3:2–3, emphasis added). Christians are dead men walking. We died with Jesus—entered into His saving death, where all the sin that condemned us was done away with. And then He raised us to new life. Christians are not people who one day will be resurrected. We are already walking in the resurrection. We have already been infused with the same Holy Spirit and received the same power that raised Jesus from the grave.

But first we died.

Last February, I flew to Edmonton for three days of meetings. Edmonton, someone once said, is not the end of the world, but you can see it from there. It is flat and barren and frozen. The day I arrived, a Sunday afternoon, the temperature was around minus forty degrees: a coldness that makes the air brittle, the ground rigid, the nights dark and long as death. Step outside, and cold needles through every inch of your clothing. Your breath plumes from your mouth, specter-like, and swarms over you.

In the night, probably around 1:00 A.M., an eighteen-month-old girl named Erika woke up. She was in bed beside her mother, who slept on. Erika, in a sleep trance perhaps, got up, walked around the house, and then somehow managed to get out the back door through the kitchen. She walked barefoot on the frozen earth, leaving footprints in the snow, tiny and delicate like the faint stain that flower petals make when crushed between the pages of a heavy book. They strew aimlessly, those footprints, a shuffling, twining pattern. They don't go far. Twenty feet from the house, Erika lay down, curled up, and died.

Her mother woke early, around five in the morning. The first thing she noticed was that Erika was missing. She felt her absence intuitively at first, an ache, a silence, a premonition. A hollowness in her own flesh. She jumped up and searched the house, calling her daughter's name. Then she saw the back door, ajar. She stepped out and saw the loops of tiny footprints stitched in the snow: round and round and round, a journey of desolation, going nowhere.

Then she saw her baby.

She ran over and picked Erika up, cradling her tight, calling her name. She took her in the house and wrapped her thick in woolen blankets. Erika was frozen hard as porcelain, blue as sky. The mother wept, shouted, prayed. "Jesus, help! Please don't let my baby die!" Somehow, she managed to phone 911. The paramedics came, and they rushed Erika and her mother to the hospital, where a team of doctors waited. Erika arrived. She was pronounced dead.

But the doctors worked anyhow. They began a painstaking process of thawing her tiny, frail, stiff body.

An astonishing thing happened next. Erika's little heart twitched, fluttered, and then began to beat with a slow, aching thrum. A moth shaking water off rain-soaked wings. A butterfly curling up out of its chrysalis. Blood, warm red blood, suffused her. It brushed color down through her limbs. Her body softened, her arms and legs unlocking out of their angular rigidity. She began to breathe.

Then Erika woke up.

That was Sunday. By the time I left on Wednesday morning, Erika had fully recovered. She was alert, hungry, smiling, laughing. Even her toes and fingers had received back their life. Her mother? She lives in a kind of reverie, permanently wonder-struck, with no prognosis of recovery.

I imagine that the moment Erika's heart started again, everything was forever altered. I don't mean this in some mawkish, fairy-tale sense. I know that Erika's mother will have moments of aggravation and anger with her daughter, have experiences typical to all parents, wishing her girl would shut the door without slamming it or clean her plate before leaving the table. But I doubt she'll ever kiss Erika good night again without a rush of dread and thanksgiving sweeping over her. I'm sure she'll never watch Erika thread a needle or pirouette in ballet class or twirl her hair on a pencil while she chats on the phone, and not want to clap her own hands in awe, leap to her own feet, exulting.

I imagine that both mother and daughter will forever carry a sense of destiny. Erika will grow up hearing the story over and over: You died, and you came alive. Dead as a stone, but even the stones shall sing. Her mother will remember all this—treasuring it in her heart, shouting it from the rooftops—even into her decrepitude, when age bends and crumples her and strips her memory clean as a bone. The bone will be that one thing unforgettable: *You died, my little girl, and now you live.* It will be more than just a pleat in their identity: It will be the very cloth out of which their identity is cut.

Erika is resurrected.

And, strange and astonishing, this: So are you. Knowing that— hearing the story over and over that you died and were raised—is meant to alter everything. It is meant to be the core and cornerstone of who you are. It is to be the reason you look up. Why should you set your heart and mind elsewhere? Because you are someone other than the person who once wore your skin, bore your name. You are now, and evermore, a new creation.

Most days, I know, you don't experience it. Most days you neither look nor feel resurrected. I don't. And my wife will tell you that I often don't act resurrected. Paul would simply say, "That's right. Right now your new life is hidden. It's not yet in the open. It is tucked up into Jesus."

Only God knows who you truly are. To everyone else, you look like…well, yourself: rumple-skinned or gristle-boned, terse or chatty, bald or shaggy, skittish or drowsy. Just you. But God knows who you really are.

In J. R. R. Tolkien's *The Lord of the Rings,* four hobbits set out from their beloved and serene home in the Shire on a perilous journey. Early on, they stop at a pub at the edge of the Shire. They meet there a hard-bitten, wind-scoured man named Strider. The locals think Strider's a vagabond, a lone and eccentric drifter. But the hobbits discover something else about him: He's a Ranger, a warrior who roams the edges of the countryside and keeps the towns safe, unknown to those whose lives his vigilance protects daily.

But that is only the first surprise about Strider. Bit by bit, as the journey deepens and becomes more dangerous, new aspects of Strider emerge. His name is really Aragorn, and he is a man of remarkable wisdom, skill, boldness. He is respected or feared in the halls of great power. But even these revelations do not prepare his fellow travelers for the most amazing truth of all: Aragorn is the hereditary heir of all Middle-earth. He is the long-awaited One. He is the supreme king, the King of kings.

Strider? That scruffy, patchy vagrant?

The very same. It was just hidden for a time.[27]

You are a new creation, an heir and coheir with Jesus Christ. The old has gone; the new has come. Only, what you are has not yet been made known. It is true, but for now it is hidden. To those unaware, you might look like anybody, like nobody. You might appear merely a taxicab driver, a homemaker, a lawyer, a 7-Eleven clerk, a vagabond, even. But the divine truth is that the old you has died, and the new you is waiting for the right moment to be revealed.

Why be heavenly-minded? The reason is that you have already died—you are already someone else.

If we need a reason to be heavenly-minded, we also need a reason *not* to be its opposite. What is its opposite? It is, simply, being earthly-minded. *Set your minds on things above*, Paul exhorts, *not on earthly things*.

Does this mean that if I'm thinking about my son's grades in school, the daffodils blooming in my garden, the muffler rusting on my car, the meeting looming midweek, that I'm not being heavenly-minded? No. It is right and fitting that we should care about such things.

In fact, there is a kind of heavenly-mindedness that makes us of no earthly good. It's the kind that breeds either indifference to or contempt for the things of earth. In Paul's first letter to Thessalonians, he deals bluntly with that. The believers there were so enraptured with the idea of Jesus coming back to whisk them to heaven that some of them had quit working. They were set on enjoying the full rights of heavenly citizenship now. Earthly toil was beneath their dignity. Paul puts an end to that thinking with one sharp warning: *If you don't work, you don't eat*. Go a few days without good old earthly food—what seed and rain and soil make, what hands have sown and gathered and prepared—and see how far you've attained to some ethereal heavenly status. You may be a citizen of heaven, but right now you're a resident of earth, and the rent still needs paying.

Be in the world, just not of it. Make your mind-set heaven, but don't shun earth. Indeed, seek to live abundantly here and now—to savor earth's good things, its sweet fruits and white waters and warm beds, to succor its needy things, its blighted fruit and brown waters and flea-infested beds.

Just never *reduce* your life's purpose to the here and now. Earthly-minded people do that. They have no reference point that's beyond the here and now or greater than the temporal and the natural. They are consumed by and immersed in *this* life in a way that makes them blind and deaf to *that* life. They never look up.

Such people, Paul says, are enemies of the Cross. What marks out such people? How do we recognize them? What things do they do? Are they child molesters, crack peddlers, slumlords, despots, terrorists?

No, not usually. Seldom is it so lurid or melodramatic. Paul simply describes them this way: "Their god is their stomach…their mind is on earthly things" (Philippians 3:19). Their appetites, in other words, rule them. What their stomach craves has the force of divine command. They have nothing to shape the way they think and act beyond what they can know, touch, taste, see, possess. Their god is their stomach, and with a god like that, the only heresy or blasphemy is the delay of gratification.

Such people are enemies of the Cross, and, Paul says, "their destiny is destruction." If the reason to be heavenly-minded is that we're dead already, the reason not to be earthly-minded is that it kills us.

Aldous Huxley's haunting novel *Brave New World* portrays an entire society that lives this way. The story is set in a behaviorally and genetically engineered caste society. The workers, factory-lined for subservience, do their menial work without grudge or grumbling, never growing weary. The elite, the genetic aristocracy, is eugenically groomed for pleasure. Their god is their stomach. Conscience and God-consciousness has been bred out of them, out of everyone. It is a race of bodies without souls.

All the machinery of the society caters to the elite. The engine that drives the machine is "happiness." Happiness is the Supreme Good, measured by the immediacy of gratification. What you crave is what you get.

In one scene, Mustapha Mond, chief controller and ideologue for Western Europe, is meeting with some of the schoolboys from the elite group. Here's the scene:

"Consider your lives," said Mustapha Mond. "Has any of you ever encountered an insurmountable obstacle?"

The question was answered by a negative silence.

"Has any of you been compelled to live through a long time-interval between the consciousness of desire and its ful-fillment?"

"Well," began one of the boys, and hesitated. "I once had to wait nearly four weeks before a girl I wanted would let me have her."

"And you felt strong emotion in consequence?"

"Horrible!"

"Horrible; precisely," said the Controller. "Our ancestors were so stupid and short-sighted that when the first reformers came along and offered to deliver them from these horrible emotions, they wouldn't have anything to do with them."[28]

The terror in Huxley's vision is that it is not even prophetic anymore; it has become merely descriptive. It's not a telescope through which we glimpse, vague and distant, a world that might come to be. It's a mirror in which we see, stark and close, a world we already know.

I know a lady whose husband walked into the house after a lengthy business trip. She stepped forward to kiss him in greeting, but then stopped. His body, stiff-shouldered, slack-legged, told her that something was wrong. He stood there, his travel bag and attaché case clutched tight in his hands, as if he were leaving, not arriving. He looked away from her, at the wall. He looked downward, at the floor. He never looked her in the eyes.

"Is something the matter?" she asked.

"I want a divorce," he said, flat-voiced, still not looking at her.

This was after twenty-five years of marriage. This was after they had given birth to and raised three healthy children. This was after they had traveled many places together, suffered many trials, seen many wonders, lain side by side in a hundred different beds. This was after they had each learned to carry, tucked up deep inside their own skin, the other's secrets and sorrows. They had laughed and cried so often over the same things that the crucible of shared emotion had molded their faces into a likeness, a resemblance like kinship.

After all this, he wanted a divorce.

"Why? What's happened?" she asked.

"I'm not happy," he said. Then, with a kind of childish imperiousness: "*I deserve* to be happy."

Their god is their stomach.

He had met someone else, it turned out. She—of course—made him happy. So he divorced his wife of twenty-five years, and he married the woman who gave him what he deserved.

That was ten years ago. Guess who's not happy now? Within a short time, he was divorced again. He lives now in loneliness and regret. It is a dangerous thing to insist that you get what you deserve. To insist on your own happiness. To make your god your stomach.

Their destiny is destruction.

His former wife said this to me: "Mark, in the first year or so after he left, there were many things I thought of doing—selfish, sinful things. But you know what kept me from doing them? Thinking that one day I will stand before God in heaven and have to explain to God why living for Him, by His strength, wasn't enough."

For you died, and your life is now hidden with Christ in God.

For their destiny is destruction.

Set your minds on things above, not on earthly things.

THIRTEEN

DO NOT LOSE HEART

R umor has it, the devil held a garage sale. On a table he laid out all the tools he had used to harass and intimidate, to entice and accuse, each marked with its price. Lust was priced dear, but not half as much as gossip. Pride had a staggering sum attached to it. But one item was priced higher than them all. It was a plain, dull, shopworn implement, no embellishments, yet it cost more than everything else taken together. "What is this thing," a customer asked the devil, "and why is it so pricey?"

"Ah," the devil said, "*this*—how I cherish this—this is the most effective tool I have. When all other things—lust, envy, greed, sloth— can't make a dent in someone, when even pride can't find a crack, this does the trick without fail. I have beaten down more saints with this one tool than with any other one on this table."

"Well, what is it?"

"Discouragement."

I'm making an assumption. The assumption is that even the happiest people—the most glass-is-half-full, look-on-the-bright-side types—get discouraged. And then there are the rest of us, who drag discouragement around like a sack of stones, constantly trying to let it go, only to find that it keeps coming back, usually with two more stones in the bag, heavier and more cumbersome than before.

Discouragement. The apostle Paul knew all about it:

> We are hard pressed on every side...perplexed...persecuted...struck down. We always carry around in our body the death of Jesus.... For we who are alive are always being given over to death. (2 Corinthians 4:8–11)

Is there a cure for this? I don't mean some magic pill that dissolves heartache in a burst of euphoria. I don't mean some potion that makes the sullen always giddy and the downhearted forever cheery. I said before that disappointment with life—even with the best things in life—is a divine conspiracy. The shadow and hollowness in all things is one way that God keeps us restless until we rest in Him. What I mean is: Is there some discipline of heart and mind that can open us up, even in the midst of life's discouragements, to a deeper source of hope and joy?

Paul thought so:

Therefore we do not lose heart. Though outwardly we are
wasting away, yet inwardly we are being renewed day by day.
For our light and momentary troubles are achieving for us an
eternal glory that far outweighs them all. So we fix our eyes
not on what is seen, but on what is unseen. For what is seen
is temporary, but what is unseen is eternal. (2 Corinthians
4:16–18)

Therefore we do not lose heart.

. Don't misunderstand. We *are* dying: hard pressed on every
side…persecuted…perplexed…struck down…always being given
over to death…outwardly wasting away. There's no way to disguise
the condition we're in.

In *Monty Python and the Holy Grail,* a slapstick spoof of the King
Arthur legend, there's a scene in which King Arthur meets the dreaded
black knight in a dark wood. The black knight, standing in foreboding
grimness, forbids him to pass.

"I come as friend, Black Knight," Arthur says. "I have no dispute
with you. I seek only the Holy Grail. Let me pass."

"None shall pass," the black knight says, ominous, hulking. "Turn
back or prepare to die."

So Arthur cuts off the black knight's right arm. Blood spurts from
the wound. "Now let me pass," he says to the black knight.

"None shall pass," the black knight says.

"But I cut your arm off," Arthur says.

"What, this?" the black knight says. "That's nothing—a mere flesh wound."

Paul suffers no such illusions. Paul doesn't pretend that losing an arm is a mere flesh wound. *I am not going to bluff you,* he says. *Life is often brutal, ugly, lonely. Bad things happen. Trouble comes. We are dying all the way to death. Outwardly, we waste away.*

Still, he says, we don't lose heart.

Why not, Paul?

Because inwardly, we are being renewed day by day.

So it comes down to this: What renews us inwardly and daily?

Before we answer, pause. Paul says that we do not lose heart because, though *outwardly* wasting away—getting sick, losing jobs, struggling in relationships, getting old—we are renewed *inwardly* day by day.

The world turns this inside out and backward. Many of us attempt, often desperately and at great cost, to be *outwardly* renewed day by day, while *inwardly* we waste away. We pour out time and money and energy to look beautiful, to have pleasure, to feel good about ourselves, to avoid suffering. Every year we spend billions of dollars on diets and gyms and cosmetics and surgeries and prescriptions and leisure crafts and getaways—all in a *vain* attempt to reverse our outward wasting. Yet the wasting relentlessly presses on, blithely and cruelly indifferent to our defenses. All the while, we wither on the inside, lonely, empty, afraid.

So the first thing, the needed thing, to do to renew ourselves inwardly day by day is to place our hope in something other than outward renewal. It's not wrong to stay fit, work out, lose weight, eat well, be healthy. It's a good idea, in fact. But if this is *what we hope in,* the battle is lost before it's joined. Face it: You are outwardly wasting away. Have you not seen yourself lately? I compare my image in the mirror today with photos of myself fifteen, twenty years ago. Where is that young, smooth-skinned man, so jaunty and lean, with that thick head of hair?

Wasted away.

But I don't lose heart. I made a decision a long time ago: My hope lies elsewhere. I accept that—after I've eaten well and exercised often, after I've flossed and scrubbed and groomed and scoured, after I've cleaned the dirt from under my fingernails and clipped the hair bristling out my ears—I am still outwardly wasting away. I live by a great *nevertheless. Nevertheless,* though I die, yet shall I live. *Nevertheless,* though the stall is empty and the fig tree does not blossom, yet will I trust. *Nevertheless,* though He slay me, yet shall I worship.

I have staked everything on being renewed inwardly day by day.

So let me ask again: *What is it* that renews us inwardly and daily?

One thing above all: being heavenly-minded.

Inwardly we are being renewed day by day. For our light and momentary troubles are achieving for us an eternal weight of glory that far outweighs them all. This is one of the most remarkable declarations in the Bible. Paul is claiming two things here, both staggering in their implications.

—⟋⟍—

The first thing Paul claims is that trouble in this life is nothing compared with the glory in the next life. What we will know and what we will be and what we will have in heaven make anything and everything on earth as light as a cotton spore and as brief as a shooting star.

Light and momentary troubles? *But Paul, didn't you just tell us that you are persecuted, perplexed, struck down, and all day, every day, given over to death? Didn't you say earlier that you've been so overwhelmed that you feel under the sentence of death? Paul, your life has been a chronicle of suffering. Aren't these things terror and tragedy?*

No. They're light and momentary troubles.

Here is the meat of it: There is nothing that you experience—good or bad—in this world that either has more substance or is longer in duration than the glory of heaven. Everything on earth is fleeting. It passes, swiftly. It dries up, shrivels up, blows away. It is born in time, ages in time, dies in time. No matter how sturdy or enduring it appears at the moment, from conception it is seeded with decay.

Look at anything around you—the chair you sit in, the walls around you, the piano or desk against the wall. Solid. But a hundred years from now? A thousand years?

Rubble and dust. Likewise, the heartache, the pain, or the stress you suffer seems so all-consuming and all-defining now. So unmovable and permanent. But it's passing away. It is light and momentary.

In the Greek, the word for light is *elaphros*. It means *easy to bear.* The death of my father is easy to bear? Only if I compare it to what's coming. Everything hinges on our willingness to fix our eyes not on what is seen, but on what is unseen. It hinges on our being heavenly-minded. Paul gives us a vivid picture of what that means:

> Now we know that if the earthly tent we live in is destroyed, we have a building from God, an eternal house in heaven, not built by human hands. Meanwhile we groan, longing to be clothed with our heavenly dwelling, because when we are clothed, we will not be found naked. For while we are in this tent, we groan and are burdened, because we do not wish to be unclothed but to be clothed with our heavenly dwelling, so that what is mortal may be swallowed up by life. Now it is God who has made us for this very purpose and has given us the Spirit as a deposit, guaranteeing what is to come.
>
> Therefore we are always confident and know that as long as we are at home in the body we are away from the Lord. We live by faith, not by sight. We are confident, I say, and would prefer to be away from the body and at home with the Lord. (2 Corinthians 5:1–8)

We're living in a tent. Naked. And groaning for home.

One spring weekend, a friend and I took our sons and two of their friends camping on the west coast of Vancouver Island. It turned out to be one of the wettest, coldest weekends of the wet and cold season. We hiked down the muddy trail in slanting gray rain, arriving at our site sodden and chilled. We set up our tents on the beach, between the edge of the forest and the tide line, tucked in behind a rough windscreen of driftwood. But the wind and the rain swooped in on us anyway, merciless. We huddled around the meager warmth of a fire that sputtered in the heavy downpour. The wetness and the sand found its way into our tents, our food, our clothes, our sleeping bags, crusting and drenching everything. We spent most of our time scratching and shivering and trying to stay warm.

And dreaming. Dreaming of our homes: the clean hotness of bath water, the comfort and warmth of dry clothes and beds, the tastiness of food that wasn't damp or gritty or burnt. We were, sure enough, miserable. But how much more deplorable our lot would have been without a clear vision of the homes to which we would soon return. There we would peel off our damp, clinging, scratchy clothes, dance in a hot shower, dress in fleece pajamas, and rest beneath a down quilt, our heads on a soft pillow. What made the camping experience bearable—light and momentary—was knowing what awaited us at home.

We're living in a tent, naked, groaning, Paul says. Waiting to get home. And that homecoming will be like life swallowing up death. Funny that Paul should put it that way. We are accustomed to think that, because we are wasting away outwardly, we tilt swiftly toward a day when death devours life, when these once agile bodies stiffen, wizen, crumple, and fall into the hungry maw of death. Isn't that what Paul said? "For we are always being given over to death"?

Listen again, Paul says. Every day you're lugging death. Living is a kind of dying. But every day, you move closer to *that day,* when life—life in all its fullness, life without taint or shadow, life innocent of sorrow—swallows up death. You don't die; you're dying now. But one day a huge and pure vitality will overtake mortality. God's life will swallow your dying as sure as the earth drinks in the rain, and fruit and flower spring forth from it.

The second thing that Paul claims is even more remarkable. He says that trouble in this life actually *achieves* for us an eternal weight of glory. The Greek word for *achieve* is *katergazomai*. It means *to make possible, to fashion, to work out* for us.

This is astounding news. Your outward wasting away, Paul says, and all that causes it, furthers it, worsens it—all these things are not just unfortunate by-products of life. They are not merely the unhappy accidents of biology, geography, chronology: being the wrong person in the wrong place at the wrong time. They are, rather, inseparable from our destiny. The trouble we're in is indispensable to the glory that awaits, raw material for a work of everlasting beauty. Earthly trouble *achieves* for us—*katergazomai*—the wonders of heaven.

It's like this. A while back, some men came and made a terrible mess behind the church where I am pastor. They hewed down trees, ripped up grass, gouged up earth, blew up rocks. They scattered rubble everywhere. They turned parkland into wasteland.

What did I do in response? I thanked them. I thanked them because the mess *made possible*—*katergazomai*—the groundwork for our new building.

A tent you can plop anywhere. It needs no foundation, leaves no scar. Pull it up, and all that remains is a soft imprint of its underside upon the earth, and soon no trace at all. But a building can start only with a mess. It calls for initial demolition, for permanent alteration. You cannot—wish as you will, try as you might—build a foundation otherwise.

In much the same way, our earthly troubles *fashion—katergazomai*—a heavenly home for us. Somehow, in God's strange smelter and smithy, eternal glory is wrought from earthly trials. Jesus said that we should store up treasures in heaven. Paul implies—as does Jesus—that the primary means for doing so is hardship. Suffering is heaven's treasure trove, its principal source of wealth.

I don't know exactly how this works, but to show what it *works out—katergazomai*—I can point to James's letter:

> Consider it pure joy, my brothers, whenever you face trials of many kinds, because you know that the testing of your faith develops perseverance. Perseverance must finish its work so that you may be mature and complete, not lacking anything. (James 1:2–4)

Or to Peter's:

> Praise be to the God and Father of our Lord Jesus Christ! In his great mercy he has given us new birth into a living hope through the resurrection of Jesus Christ from the dead, and

into an inheritance that can never perish, spoil or fade—kept in heaven for you.

In this you greatly rejoice, though now for a little while you may have had to suffer grief in all kinds of trials. These have come so that your faith—of greater worth than gold, which perishes even though refined by fire—may be proved genuine and may result in praise, glory and honor when Jesus Christ is revealed. (1 Peter 1:3–4, 6–7)

Trouble *works out* in us the character of Jesus Christ—the one who Himself learned obedience through what He suffered (see Hebrews 5:8). Imagine it: Jesus, the unblemished one, whose life flowed in a seamless rhythm of divine imitation, learning obedience, and learning it through loss and strife and wounds.

Few things have the power to *fashion* in us utter trust in God and deep conformity to the character of Jesus Christ like suffering does. Few things build our faith and refine our faith like it does. What others intend for evil, God uses for good. He takes trials of many kinds and from them *makes possible* in us the heart of His Son. And to become like Christ is our everlasting destiny. Thus, such trials *achieve* for us an eternal glory that far outweighs all else.[29]

Jesus told a parable about it. There's a rich man—tradition says that his name's Dives—and at his gate sits a beggar named Lazarus. Lazarus is a ruin of open sores and wilted flesh. He spends his days in the futile hope that the rich man will have mercy and bring him just the bones and crumbs from his lavish meals. But Dives never does.

Dogs have pity on Lazarus, but Dives does not. He lives in undiminished luxury, an orgy of self-indulgence.

Then they both die. Dives goes to hell, Lazarus to heaven. Now Dives is the beggar, the tormented one, and Lazarus receives comfort. Dives sees Father Abraham across the great divide between hell and heaven, and he begs for mercy. Abraham replies with stark logic: "Son, remember that in your lifetime you received your good things, while Lazarus received bad things, but now he is comforted here and you are in agony" (Luke 16:25).

Remember that in your lifetime you received your good things, but now you are in agony.

What startles me most in this startling story is one phrase: *your good things*. Actually, what startles me is one word: *your.* There is in store for us, all of us, good things: *your* good things. That part is fixed. What we have a role in deciding is whether or not we seek to receive all those good things in this lifetime—*Father, give me my inheritance*—or whether we are willing, for the sake of something bigger, to store up our treasure in heaven.

Where are *your* good things?

Richard Adams's novel *Watership Down* is a children's story that transcends its genre. It is a tale of rabbits, but it is really a Homeric epic, an Odyssey-like story of exile and peril and homecoming.

A warren of rabbits undertake a journey. It is meant to be a journey from danger to safety, but it becomes a journey through danger and into danger. Along the way, in moments of pining boredom or looming threat, one of the rabbits, Dandelion, tells stories to the others. The stories are mostly about the legendary rabbit El-ahrairah, a trickster-hero. El-ahrairah has uncanny shrewdness and unsheering nerves, but he always, always uses this cleverness and boldness for the sake of the people he leads—to protect them, feed them, shelter them.

In one of Dandelion's last stories about El-ahrairah, just before his own warren of rabbits face their own direst challenge, El-ahrairah ends up in a double bind. His entire warren is under threat of utter destruction, and he makes a solitary decision: to go to the Black Rabbit of Inlé, the ruler of the underworld, and sacrifice himself for the sake of his warren. So El-ahrairah goes. The Black Rabbit accepts the bargain, and is ruthless in exacting it. He mutilates and humiliates El-ahrairah: He tears off his ears, severs his tail, plucks out his whiskers, and then sends him dragging his bloodied, mangled body home.

It takes many months for El-ahrairah to find his way there. When he does, he returns to a community that is well fed, thriving, living in peace and comfort—saved by his sacrifice. But no one cares, no one notices. They ignore him. Some even mock him.

In the cool of evening, El-ahrairah stands at the field's edge. Lord Frith, the supreme ruler of the rabbits, gently comes alongside him. This is the scene:

> As the light began to fail, he suddenly realized that Lord Frith
> was close beside him, among the leaves.

"Are you angry, El-ahrairah?" asked Lord Frith.

"No, my lord," replied El-ahrairah. "I am not angry. But I have learned that with creatures one loves, suffering is not the only thing for which one may pity them. A rabbit who does not know when a gift has been given him is poorer than a slug, even though he may think otherwise."

"Wisdom is found on the desolate hillside, El-ahrairah, where none comes to feed, and the stony bank where the rabbit scratches a hole in vain. But speaking of gifts, I have a few trifles for you...."

And with that, Lord Frith restores El-ahrairah to a state surpassing what he ever knew before.[30]

For his light and momentary troubles achieve for him an eternal weight of glory that far outweighs them all.

Do not lose heart.

Now You Do It!

D r. Klaus Bockmuehl was a small man, and intense. He could be gruff, imperious even, a man standing in the midst of storm or war, whose job it was to sort us out. There was a crosshatch of ruptured veins along the ridges of his jawbone—symptoms of his body's struggle, I imagine, to contain him. But he was a patient man too. Often I saw him leaning his head in close, nodding slowly, listening carefully to the ill-formed question of some meek student.

He had a sharp and quick mind that could nimbly parse an idea down to its grammatical minutiae, tease out its most hidden assumptions. But what I remember most was his voice. It had a vigor disproportionate to his body's size. Even later, when his sickness made him ghoulishly thin, that voice stayed intact, with its booming depth.

He would be lecturing on, say, the Hegelian presuppositions of the nineteenth-century Tübingen School of Theology, his reasoning intricate and flawless, yet his voice alone could carry the argument: It had its own force of logic, its own quality of indisputableness. If Dr. Bockmuehl said that Frederich Schleiremacher was pandering to the overbred and sentimental upper class of his day, or that Albrecht Ritschl was laying the ground for a Kingless kingdom, and he said it with *that voice*—it must be so. Who would gainsay it? The apostle Peter writes, "If anyone speaks, he should do it as one speaking the very words of God" (1 Peter 4:11). Dr. Klaus Bockmuehl is my default picture for this verse.

Dr. Bockmuehl was professor of Biblical and Historical Theology at Regent College. His colleagues were the likes of J. I. Packer and Gordon Fee and Bruce Waltke, men who themselves possessed, and carried with magnificent authority, an almost impossibly large storehouse of comprehension. How did anyone read and write that many books, and still have time for a day job? How did they keep at their fingertips such encyclopedic knowledge—such overflowing caches of lore and insight and arcanum, all ready to be articulated, at the merest prompting, in crystalline, elegant, and passionate oratory—and still have time to tie their shoes, drive their cars, talk on phones, sleep and eat? Beside such men, the brightest student became tongue-tied. This was Bockmuehl's company. There he stood, stout and burly next to Packer's gangling skinniness or Fee's swaggering tallness, but he held his own, and usually then some.

He was a favorite with the students. Demanding, exacting, rigorous, he was also childlike in faith. And he was in love—with God, with God's Word and God's ways, with his beloved wife, Elisabeth, with his children (who were staggeringly intelligent like he was), with his students. When he stood up to speak of God, the love of God compelled him. He never recovered from the thrill that God had raised him up for such a task. He never tired of it.

I was Dr. Bockmuehl's teaching assistant the year he died. When he asked me to assist him, he didn't know he was dying. He thought that the cancer he had been diagnosed with two years earlier was gone, cut clean out and burned straight through. He brought me on to do the typical things T.A.'s do—grading papers, running errands, proctoring exams, being a first contact for puzzled or aggrieved students, and the general sifting and sorting of professorial debris—but he also hired me to edit his writing. He had just begun a new book, later published under the title *Listening to the God Who Speaks*. He would write, and I would, chapter by chapter, smooth the rough Germanic edges of his prose.

Not long after I began working with him, he got the news: The sickness was back, thick, wild, aggressive. Back with a vengeance. Back to finish the job.

With that news, my responsibilities changed. Dr. Bockmuehl couldn't continue lecturing, and so his classes were conducted as audio or video courses. I got far more involved in his students' personal and academic lives than was traditionally part of the role of a T.A. Under J. I. Packer's watchful, imposing eye, I graded all the papers, even the research ones. I led Dr. Bockmuehl's student group.

And I edited his book. That was his last obsession, his parting gift to the world. The book is not an academic treatise; it is a personal and theological reflection on God's intimate guidance. This was the fruit of his many years of scholarship. This was the prize. After mastering the intricacies and conundrums of two millennia of theological inquiry and disquisition, after becoming an authority on the biographies and histories of dozens of theologians, famous and obscure, after spending half a lifetime immersed in the complexities of God's ways with man and man's ways with God, the conclusion of the matter was: *Listen, and do whatever He tells you* (see John 2:5). Thousands of books read and pondered. Thousands of student papers assigned and critiqued. Hundreds of lectures prepared and delivered. Dozens of books and articles researched and written. All gathered up and boiled down, it came to this: "He who has an ear, let him hear what the Spirit says" (Revelation 2:7).

He almost didn't finish the book. His health wasted quickly. His stockiness gave way, overnight it seemed, to brittleness. His breath thinned, as if some cruel, strong hand were clamping down a valve on it. He slept most of the day. He ate little. Simple tasks—climbing the stairs, finding a book, making conversation—had become hugely wearisome, a dread to contemplate, let alone perform.

Once a week I went to his home to pick up what he had managed, in dwindling strength, to write. Elisabeth would let me in. I would sit in their small living room, made even smaller by the walls of books that were stacked floor to ceiling and corner to corner. I read the titles as I waited: Heidegger's *Being and Time,* Barth's *Church Dogmatics,*

Niebuhr's *Moral Man and Immoral Society,* Bonhoeffer's *Letters and Papers from Prison,* histories of the Church Fathers, the Scholastics, the Pietists, the Revivalists, the Reformers, the classic writings of Aquinas and Anselm and Augustine, the novels of Günter Grass and Leo Tolstoy and Arnold Bennett, the poetry of Milton and Spenser and Keats, thick works of philosophy, philology, phenomenology, physics, metaphysics.

Muffled voices upstairs. A dull thump on the floor above. A scuffle of feet on the stairs. And then there he was, thinner and paler than the week before. A wet rattling sound in his chest, like a sodden stick caught in the spokes of a spun wheel, amplified in his breathing. Elisabeth would ease him down into his chair, and he'd sit still and silent for a minute, gathering breath, gathering strength. Then he'd speak. It was always the same voice, deep and sure, a thunder that rushed into the space where lightning had burned up the air.

He always asked how I was doing. As if I was the one whose well-being mattered most here. But, to him, that was exactly right. He was the one dying. His hours were battlefields. Each day was an English Channel that he swam, and each day the water got darker, colder, rougher. Within months, maybe weeks, he would throw his last gasping, exhausted stroke, and go down. He now longed for that. Living had become too onerous. Every day, forever got closer. He had lived a life of worship and kingdom-devotion. He knew his God. For him, to live was Christ, to die gain. He was heaven-bent. He couldn't wait. Finish the book—that's all he wanted. Finish the book, and let go.

But me? I was going to live for now, for good or for ill. I was still earth bound. That's why he asked how I was. His work was almost done. Mine, just starting.

One day on one of our visits, I asked him what it had been like knowing Karl Barth. Dr. Bockmuehl had, many years before, had a personal association with the redoubtable Swiss theologian, who had done so much to reestablish the authority of Scripture and the sovereignty of God in a theological world rotted through with liberalism. Dr. Bockmuehl told me one story.

"I saw Barth many years ago," he said. "I sat with him, wondering what to say. Then I thought to pay him honor. So I said, 'Dr. Barth, you have done so much to turn back the tides of liberalism. When you are gone, I pray that God will raise up another to do what you have done.' Barth fixed me with his eyes."

Bockmuehl fixed me with his eyes.

"'No, don't pray that,' he said. 'You do it.'"

I was on an island when he died, visiting, along with some other students, Loren and Mary-Ruth Wilkinson, both Regent profs. It was June, and the weather was clear and warm. I had been canoeing, and came in to rest. It was early evening. The phone rang, and Loren answered. He listened, stoic. "I see," he said. "Thank you for calling."

He came into the large open room where a number of students sat, chatting. "That was Elisabeth," he said. "Klaus died this morning."

I went to my room, and read the Psalms, and wept.

Hundreds of people filled the stone church of St. John's Anglican in Shaugnessy, Vancouver, for his memorial service. Dr. James Houston gave the address. It was then I learned Dr. Bockmuehl's dying words. In a voice that stayed strong to the end, he looked at his beloved Elisabeth, and then at his children, and said, "I know that my redeemer liveth." And he died.

I often have pictured myself there. Not that I had any right to be, but I picture it anyhow. I entered pastoral ministry in part because Dr. Bockmuehl, in one of his dying conversations with me, delivered a word so startling that I came to understand it as a word of prophecy. My plans had been to teach literature and writing at a local college after graduation. Dr. Bockmuehl had always asked how my search for work was going. After one discouraging week, I told him not so well. "Well," he said, in his brusque Germanic way, "don't turn your back on the church if they should come calling."

Two months after he died, the church came calling. Out of the blue, a pastor three hundred miles away phoned me and asked if I would join him on staff. If not for Dr. Bockmuehl's gruff and blunt admonishment still raw in me like a branding, I likely would have said no.

So I picture myself by the bedside. And in my mind he adds one thing, one phrase, to his parting speech. "I know that my redeemer liveth," he says, and says it in *that voice,* so that there's no possibility of doubting or gainsaying it. Then somehow he manages to look at each and all who are there, to singularly fix us all in the stare of those piercing gray eyes.

"Now you do it."

PART IV

Heaven-Bent: Living in Light of Forever

FOURTEEN

BIG DEAL

F ew words capture more starkly the impasse between heaven and earth than these: "Precious in the sight of the Lord is the death of his saints" (Psalm 116:15). In a culture stricken with the "Thanatos Syndrome"—a hybrid virus that mixes a dread of death with a lust for it—such verses come as ancient enigmas, hieroglyphs without a Rosetta stone to unlock them.[31]

Death startles and bewilders us. And so, as cause or consequence, we've lost the idea of the good death. To past generations of Christians—to the Puritans as a preeminent example—the good death was at the very heart of their belief about the good life. The good life was life lived in preparation for a good death—meaning not death eased by the best in palliative care, but death faced with thankfulness and boldness and humility. One could not live well before God, with God, within community, apart from deep reflection on the meaning of death and a prayerful readiness for it.

Earlier Christians were, in many ways, more preoccupied with the question of their death-style than their lifestyle. Margaret Kim Peterson, commenting on the consensus of Christian thinkers from Basil the Great in the fourth century, to Martin Luther in the sixteenth, to Jeremy Taylor in the seventeenth, sums up their wisdom on this matter: "Don't let an event as important as death take you by surprise." She goes on to describe how she and her husband, Hyung Goo Kim, had to do this literally: He died of AIDS in 1995. She writes:

> As my husband's health began to fail, we began to make preparations for his death. We made wills, we met a funeral director, and we bought a cemetery plot. We decided that we wanted the stone marker on his grave already there when he was buried, and so we selected a stone and had it engraved and set in place.... When we visited the cemetery to see my husband's newly laid gravestone, we took a picture of him next to his gravestone. He is sitting cross-legged on the ground, looking straight into the camera, and in front of him is a flat stone with the legend, "I know that my redeemer liveth," and under it his name and the year of his birth, with a space next to it for the year of his death. It is a photograph at once macabre, and darkly funny, and soberly realistic. He is dying, and he knows it, and he also knows that his redeemer lives, and that he is soon to see him face to face. Isn't this how a Christian ought to live, and ought to die?[32]

To prepare for a good death doesn't mean that you live for death. It is not a death wish—a longing for or fascination with morbidity. Rather, it means to live life so that death comes as a *completion,* not merely an ending. Such a death-style is, actually, a vigorous yearning for life, for life to the full. Those who sit cross-legged before their own tombstone are free to savor earth's goodness and bind its wounds. They have been lastingly disabused of the idea that this world is their home. They are often of much earthly good. In the shadow of the tombstone, the sky shimmers bright.

A man I know nearly drowned off the Oregon coast. He was a strong swimmer, familiar with the waters. But the waters there shape-shift. They're capricious and treacherous, and a wrenching undertow pulled him down and pulled him out. Soon the shoreline was a thin black line, far away, and his body was dead weight from panic, struggle, fear. He bored down one last time and, miraculously, found himself groping sandy bottom, the froth of the surf falling off him like blossoms. It was nightfall. He staggered along the beach, disoriented. He saw a light. A house. He stumbled to it. People. A warm blanket. Hot coffee. Food.

He had never felt more alive. He savored everything—the coffee, the warmth, the light, the food, the care. He savored the fullness of life: what life is in its essence, uncluttered by boredom, busyness, dullness, cynicism, ingratitude. Everything was good and clean, like the creation sprung fresh from the voice of God. This was life as God made it, pure, new, full.

Being aware of death makes us more aware of life. It keeps our appetites healthy, our wonderment sharp. It winnows clutter from our life. From the perspective of death, we learn to order our lives differently. "Teach us to number our days aright," Moses once prayed, "that we may gain a heart of wisdom" (Psalm 90:12). *Teach us to pray. Teach us Your ways. Teach us to number our days.*

Some knowledge, some skill, has leached out of us, if ever it was in us. Now we must be taught it, and God Himself must be the principal teacher. On our own, we don't know how to number a day. It is abstruse as calculus, cryptic as quantum mechanics. On our own, days are no more than a random accumulation of *chronos*, rocks in a sack, rags in a pile. We plod through unnumbered days, check them off on a calendar, scratch them into a stone wall. We *get through* them, but rarely *live in* them. A numbered day, by contrast, is one lived in attentiveness and thankfulness, one we've named, received, entered. This, Moses says, it necessary for gaining a heart of wisdom. Apart from it, we will be dull-hearted or hard-hearted or half-hearted.

We learn to number our days aright by thinking about our death. "You sweep men away in the sleep of death," Moses says. "They are like the new grass of the morning—though in the morning it springs up new, by evening it is dry and withered" (Psalm 90:5–6). Only a steady gaze at the brevity and frailty of our own existence can snap us out of the monotony of unnumbered days. Only an unflinching recognition of death's power to make all new things old, all supple things brittle, all solid things dust, can break *chronos*'s spell. Rumors of death awaken a sense of *kairos* time, a desire to live life on purpose.

And news of our mortality helps us see things in their right proportion, their real shape, their true meaning. Shattering defeats, spectacular triumphs—neither is quite what it seems when viewed from the graveyard. And the often staggering but mostly hidden value of ordinary things—food, light, warmth, love—shines through. We receive these small wonders again as gifts and holy surprises.

Here's the gist: Death, carefully pondered, resolutely faced, actually looses its grip on us, its deadlock on our imaginations. It can wholly reawaken holy wonder. We learn to cherish those things we often take for granted: lying beneath a huge sky alongside a child, searching out shapes in clouds; the taste of freshly picked carrots with the dirt only brushed off; the prickly, tickling feel of cat's whiskers on your leg; the sound of rain plinking down metal pipes at night. And the things we often seek after desperately—recognition for a contract deal, more money, a holiday on a luxury cruiser, five minutes alone with *that* woman—become to us nothing, detritus underfoot, smoke in the eyes.

"Death in the morning," the eighteenth-century lexicographer Dr. Johnson said, "powerfully clears the mind." This is true when we face our own death. It is also true when we face the death of those we love. Never are we so keen to sort out the substance of life from its excess and its residue than when a loved one is dying. Death has a unique power—greater than worship or prayer or the joyfulness of homecoming—to set us trembling and hungry in the presence of God.

Luke tells the story of Jairus, whose only daughter, twelve years old, is dying (see Luke 8:40–56). Jairus is the synagogue ruler in

Capernaum. It makes you wonder. A synagogue ruler, yet. How often has Jairus, busy with his important work, forgotten his daughter? So many people want to see him, be seen with him. So many lunch meetings. So many committee meetings. Imagine a typical conversation with his wife: "Honey, please understand. If I just work a bit harder, they'll notice me in Jerusalem. Don't you see where this could lead? It won't be forever, I promise. In two weeks, I promise, my schedule will clear up a bit. And next year, we'll take a real holiday. I promise."

But now his only child is dying. And what would he not give to have her well? He would give anything. The title. The reputation. The prestige. The money. The whole lot.

Timothy Jones writes:

Awareness of death…has not only framed how I look at life. It has also begun to work a change in how I walk through life. It has, in other words, brought not just new meaning to my moments, but changes to my behavior…. Our awareness of the transitoriness of life, I find, concentrates my priorities, helps me refashion my daily choices.[33]

For Jairus, the prospect of his only child dying concentrated his priorities, helped refashion his daily choices. The self-important synagogue ruler was suddenly the desperate father, a man falling at the feet of Jesus, pleading with Him. Maybe last week, Jairus sat with scowling, gloomy men on an emergency committee appointed to debate the question, "What shall we do about Jesus? How shall we handle this dangerous young upstart?" But death has a power to concentrate priorities—to bring us pleading to the feet of Jesus.

On a flight to Calgary I found myself sitting beside a woman I knew. We'd gone to the same church, years before, when she was still a girl. Back then, she loved Christ, loved His people. She told me, as we flew over the Rockies, that she'd left all that behind. She was now living with a man. She hadn't been near a church in years. She had no interest in all that "God stuff." I asked her why.

"Well," she said, "let's be honest: Church is boring."

Too often it's true. Somehow, by some reverse alchemy, we've turned gold into slag. We've taken the most dramatic, exhilarating news there could ever be—that the God of heaven and earth came looking for you and me, scouring every dungeon and prison and slave market to find us while we were still His enemy, came to rescue us, to pay our ransom by His own sacrifice, to adopt us as sons and daughters and appoint us as heralds—and we've made it boring. Surely no greater feat has ever been wrought on the face of the earth, in the history of the world, than to reduce such magnificence to banality and blandness.

"Yes," I said to the woman, "sometimes it is. But tell me, what do you do now? What isn't boring? What's exciting?"

"I go to the nightclubs. To bars. To parties."

"Oh," I said.

She thought I was shocked and offended, to hear of a former choirgirl in such places: *Nightclubs! Bars! Parties!*

"It's no big deal," she said defensively. "Going to a nightclub or a bar: It's no big deal. That's the trouble with Christians. They always think it's such a big deal. But it's no big deal at all."

"Yes," I said. "I was thinking that myself. It's no big deal at all."

Too much of our life is no big deal at all. "What is man," the psalmist asks God, wonder-struck, "that you are mindful of him...? You made him a little lower than the heavenly beings and crowned him with glory and honor" (Psalm 8:4–5). We're in a class just beneath the angels, glory encircling us, honor radiating from us. And yet many of us spend our lives in trivial pursuit, chasing small thrills, trying to stave off boredom. A treadmill occasionally relieved by a carnival. No big deal.

A better death-style might be just the tonic we need. "I press on to take hold of that for which Christ Jesus took hold of me," Paul said (Philippians 3:12). But his clarity about this likely had to do with the fact that, as he wrote, he sat crossed-legged in front of his own tombstone. He faced the prospect of his own death squarely. And what did he conclude? "For to me, to live is Christ and to die is gain" (Philippians 1:21).

To live is Christ; to die is gain. That's a big deal. And those two things, the living and the dying, go together. Each interprets the other. Imagine that Paul had said, "For to me, to live is nightclubs. To live is stocks and bonds. To live is golf." Then to die is always loss. But because Paul lived his life in pursuit of a big deal—to live *is* Christ—he was able to see death as gain. And because he looked, unflinching, at death, he wasn't easily distracted from life's true purpose. To live is *Christ.*

Paul isn't speaking in some aloof academic manner when he says that. He isn't the pedant behind the lectern, the preacher in his gowns. He isn't like I am right now, the writer in his houserobe, a cup of fresh-perked coffee steaming by his elbow, line after line shuttling across his computer screen like lacework. Paul writes from a prison cell, beneath the gathering shadow of approaching death. But he knows—not in spite of that, but because of it—what the big deal is. He knows that his death might be *at* the hands of Rome—or cancer, or an aneurysm, or an industrial accident—but his life is never *in* the hands of anything or anyone but God.

Paul knows how to number his days aright. He knows to celebrate simple and ordinary things. "Rejoice!" he says, as though his favorite football team just won the bowl. But, of course, it's better, infinitely better, than that. "I will say it again: Rejoice!"

"I have learned," he says a little further on, "the secret of being content…whether living in plenty or in want. I can do everything through him who gives me strength" (Philippians 4:4, 12–13).

That's a big deal.

FIFTEEN

WAX ON, WAX OFF

T he perspective on life you get from the graveyard is a good one. It's necessary, salutary. But it's not the best one. That perspective comes from the eternal city. We need more than a lifestyle. We need even more than a death-style. We need a heaven-style. The philosopher Heidegger described human existence as "living toward death." But the Christian's existence is living toward eternity, where death is only eternity's gateway. "We cannot," Timothy Jones writes, "live rightly until we aim *past* life. Eternity provides the only goal that makes ultimate sense of our lives."[34]

As a child, I was fascinated by those men, fierce and taut, who broke stacks of bricks, slabs of ice, layers of planks, with their bare hands, their naked heads. The brute force amazed me. I tried and tried to do it myself, but only came away with stinging skin and aching bone. Then I learned that what was needed was not animal power, but a simple technique coupled with concentration: *You have to aim past what you're hitting.* That way, your momentum and strength are poised to carry through the object rather than end at the object. The bricks buckle and crumble, the ice cracks and shatters, the boards splinter and snap. But you have to aim past.

That's what this entire book has been about: aiming past life. Fixing our minds and hearts on things above. Fixing our eyes, not on what is seen and temporal, but on what is unseen and eternal. Acknowledging—yes, celebrating—that this world is not enough. You're heaven-bent. Live that way, and all your momentum, all your force, is poised to break through.

That's what Paul was doing in prison. He tells the Philippian believers what the big deal is: To live is Christ, to die is gain. He tells them about his passion for pursuing this: "I press on to take hold of that for which Christ Jesus took hold of me" (Philippians 3:12). Then he discloses the technique: Aim past life. "Forgetting what is behind and straining toward what is ahead, I press on toward the goal to win the prize for which God has called me heavenward in Christ Jesus" (vv. 13–14).

The Karate Kid is a 1980s movie about a skinny, skittish boy named Daniel who moves from New Jersey to Los Angeles and gets roughed up and ostracized by the local toughs. Daniel wants to learn karate for self-defense and retaliation. He asks Mr. Miyagi, the old Japanese gardener at his apartment complex, to apprentice him. Mr. Miyagi is reluctant, but finally he agrees and invites Daniel to come to his house the next morning. Early.

Daniel arrives at daybreak, eager and jaunty, ready to spar. Mr. Miyagi takes him out behind his house. There sits a fleet of classic cars, their paint dull. "If you want to learn karate, first you must wax cars, Daniel. I show you." He demonstrates a vigorous circular motion, clockwise with the right hand, counterclockwise with the left. "See, Daniel: Wax on. Wax off. Like this: With right hand, wax on; with left hand, wax off." He hands the rags and wax to Daniel, and walks away, muttering, "Wax on. Wax off," his own hands inscribing and burnishing the air.

That's how Daniel spends the first day. Mr. Miyagi invites him to come back and learn karate the next morning. Early.

Daniel shows up, less jaunty, but still eager. Mr. Miyagi gives him another menial job to do. These jobs, he explains, are in exchange for the karate lessons. So that's the routine: Every morning Daniel shows up ready to learn karate, and every morning Mr. Miyagi loads him with another huge chore: first the cars, then painting both sides of the six-foot fence that winds around Mr. Miyagi's large yard, then sanding to a silky smoothness his sprawling layers of deck.

Always, Mr. Miyagi is very picky, very particular—the work must be done in a certain way. Not only must the cars be waxed and polished in broad, circular swoops, but the fence must be painted in sweeping, wrist-cocking strokes, and the sanding done in a short, tight scrubbing motion.

Daniel works to exhaustion. On the night he finishes the sanding, Mr. Miyagi walks into his yard whistling. Fresh-caught fish flop and glitter at his side. Daniel stands up, sweaty, weary, angry, and stands the old man down. "You told me you'd teach me karate. And all you've done is made me your slave. I quit!" Daniel starts to walk away.

"Daniel-san," Mr. Miyagi says.

"What?"

"Come here, Daniel-san." The sheer commanding force in the old gardener's voice stops Daniel in his tracks. He swaggers back, sullen and defiant, and stands in insolent looseness before the old man.

"Daniel-san, show me wax on and wax off."

Daniel, sulkily, lazily, shows him the circular hand motions.

"No, Daniel-san! Not like that!" There's fire in Mr. Miyagi's voice—steel, threat. Daniel straightens up. He does it again, obedient this time, sweeping through the motions with precision, force, focus.

"Good. Now show me paint fence."

Daniel does it listlessly. Mr. Miyagi explodes: "No, Daniel-san! Show me paint fence!" Mr. Miyagi grabs Daniel's floppy arms and forces the regimen with swiftness and hardness. "Now show me sand deck!" Daniel does, not daring now to get it wrong.

Then Mr. Miyagi begins to punch and kick at him. Daniel, to his amazement—with the motions of waxing car, painting fence, sanding deck—blocks every hit.

He has been in secret apprenticeship. He's learned karate unawares.

It's something like that with us. Often we wonder what use our work is—it's dreary, and wearying, and seems devoid of higher purpose. Often we wonder why God is so picky about doing it *this* way rather than some other way that seems easier, less painful, less boring, more engaging. Often, we are bewildered by life's bursts of stunningly hurtful events mixed together with its long stretches of numbing uneventfulness.

It's secret apprenticeship. One day we will discover that we have learned heaven's ways unaware. The throats we rubbed raw trying to teach our classrooms full of defiant, unruly children were being warmed up to sing God's praise with the hosts of heaven. The muscles we bruised and tore digging ditches, hauling stones, lugging groceries, were being limbered up to dance before the throne. The heart that was, again and again, broken was being made pure and deep for the day of its filling.

A couple from my church recently gave me a copy of the eulogy read at their sister's funeral. Kathy Merill had spent her life in Taiwan running the Door of Hope, a home and school for girls whose parents had died or, because of poverty, could no longer support their daughters. Kathy had become these girls' "mother." For forty years she taught and cared for hundreds of them.

Wax on, wax off, paint fence, sand deck.

When Kathy finally retired, she moved back to her hometown in California to live in a small apartment on her very modest income. But only a few months after returning, she was dead. Cancer. It riddled through her, and it took her down, swift and merciless.

Lorna Chao was one of the girls Kathy had raised. She's now a wife and mother. She gave the eulogy at Kathy's funeral, and she concluded her funny and personal and deeply moving testimony of Kathy's life with this:

I want to mention one thought that has brought a lot of comfort to me in the past couple of weeks while I struggled through the loss…. That's the memory of Kathy's last several hours. On the last night before Miss Merill passed away, we were by her side; we sang hymns, recited verses, prayed and talked to her until early morning as she drifted in and out of consciousness. My husband, Sam, asked her two questions: "Kathy, do you believe you are going to receive a crown as reward from God?" She nodded. "Kathy, do you have any pain?" She shook her head.

After Sam gave her the benediction, I decided to do something I always wanted to do but never had the chance or the guts. I held her hands and said to her, "Kathy, I and all the girls from the Door of Hope want you to know something: We love you very much and we appreciate you a lot. You have blessed our lives, and among all the gifts you gave us, the best one is the gospel. Thank you for bringing us to Christ." Then I said something like this: "You know what? Even though you have never married, God has blessed you with hundreds of kids. At least when it comes to the number of children, you sure have beaten every other woman." Then, to my astonishment, she laughed! That big smile could be easily detected even under her oxygen mask.

It might be the last smile she had on earth, but I am sure there are numerous coming. She will smile when God says to her, "Well done, good and faithful servant. Come and share your Master's happiness." She will smile when she sees us carry on her task, bringing the gospel to unbelievers, drawing people closer to God, lifting up the weak, comforting the hurting, and giving ourselves to those less privileged. This is what she was doing all her life.[35]

All her life, she was aiming past it.

SIXTEEN

NOW DISMISS YOUR SERVANT IN PEACE

NOW THERE WAS A MAN in Jerusalem called Simeon, who was righteous and devout. He was waiting for the consolation of Israel, and the Holy Spirit was upon him. It had been revealed to him by the Holy Spirit that he would not die before he had seen the Lord's Christ. Moved by the Spirit, he went into the temple courts. When the parents brought in the child Jesus to do for him what the custom of the Law required, Simeon took him in his arms and praised God, saying:

> "Sovereign Lord, as you have promised, you now dismiss your servant in peace. For my eyes have seen your salvation, which you have prepared in the sight of all people, a light for revelation to the Gentiles and for glory to your people Israel."

The child's father and mother marveled at what was said about him. Then Simeon blessed them and said to Mary, his mother: "This child is destined to cause the falling and rising of many in Israel, and to be a sign that will be spoken against, so that the thoughts of many hearts will be revealed. And a sword will pierce your own soul too."

LUKE 2:25–35

T his day, I imagine, started like any other. The same problem, only a bit worse: how to get these old bones unstuck and this inert flesh moving. How to stir this blood, silted-up like a river mouth, so it flows from roots to tips. Every breath gathered up carefully and rationed out sparingly. Every move precarious as trapeze work. You become a miser of your energy, your failing strength. A friend of his stepped the wrong way off a doorsill last month, and his hip popped out like a turnip pulled from slightly stubborn earth.

And the memory—*oy vey!* That is a maze-way of both clutter and emptiness. Things from earliest childhood he recalls with extraordinary vividness: the brilliant sharp blue of a prayer shawl his father kept, the shape of his mother's face as she bent close to kiss him, its soft oval like something hand-carved, or the funny way his uncle Zak used to laugh, a gulping, wheezing whoop that more than once he mistook for choking. But now he might walk into a room and forget why he's there. Or even where he is. Daylight can be more disorienting than a sandstorm, and night deeper than loneliness.

So routines are important. At 9:00, eat something. At 10:00, take a walk. At 11:00, eat something. At noon, take a nap. On Mondays, go to market. On Tuesdays, weed the garden. On Wednesdays, visit friends. And so on.

This day, I imagine, started like any other. But soon it was disrupted. The Voice, both intimate and urgent, gentle but commanding, the Voice he'd learned to trust without even a twinge of hesitation—that Voice told him to go to the temple. It broke the routine, but so be it. The Voice had revealed to him, many years ago now, that he would not die until he had seen the Lord's Christ.

Is this day that day?

Through the years, he had seen many things. He'd seen his own children become middle-aged, and their children become adults. He'd seen Rome grow in power, and arrogance, and ruthlessness. He'd seen strange religions seep in from East and West. He'd seen the religious establishment in Judea become more corrupt, kowtowing, fragmented, factionalized. He'd seen fanatical bands of zealots rise up around yet another slogan-shouting, sword-wielding firebrand, only to watch Rome crush them like insects scuttling out from beneath a stone, and nail the leader, flayed and mangled, to a gibbet.

You will not die until you've seen the Lord's anointed. He's cherished that promise, against all sorrow, loss, reversal, doubt. So there he is, hurrying off to the temple, astoundingly spry, nearly running, brooking no further interruption, thinking: *Maybe this day is that day.*

—m—

This day is that day. A mother woke this morning, and fed her child. I imagine she trembled a little inside. This day is *that* day—forty days after her baby was born. According to the Law, today she and her husband must take their son to the temple to consecrate him. Rich people buy a lamb and a dove for this occasion. But they're not rich. Her husband makes tables and chairs. Thankfully, the Law allows them to bring pigeons as a substitute.

They can't afford the lamb.

She's nervous. She's shy. Doesn't particularly like crowds. Hates when the attention's on her. But this is what the Law requires. She and her husband always do what the Law requires. Always. There's safety in that. There's a rhythm, though sometimes it's hard and stern and unrelenting, making few concessions for the weak, the slow, the heavy-burdened. But it's the Law.

So they bundle up the child and walk, slow and steady, to the temple, thinking: *This day is that day.*

You will not die until you have seen the Lord's Christ. It had been such a clear conviction. Unmistakable. It had changed everything. All those things that can wear a man down, erode him a day at a time, make his life a slow accumulation of regret and dismay—they all lost their power over him after that.

Still, there were times when he must have wondered, *Did I hear right?* It was just that he was getting so old. Rickety-boned, wizened-up, dim-eyed, dull-eared. Last spring, he'd almost died. Something inside him twisted and hardened, and for two weeks he was delirious with pain. He thought he was going to die. He almost wanted to. *But what about the Voice?*

The Voice was what kept Simeon alive. The promise. The conviction, deeper than his worst days, that he wasn't mistaken. He had heard right.

And then on this day, the Spirit says go, and Simeon goes. And on this same day, the Law says go, and Mary and Joseph go. The old Spirit-filled, Spirit-led man—the man who hears the Voice; the poor, rule-abiding young couple—the couple who heeds the Law. Both are obedient to something beyond themselves, outside of themselves, larger than themselves. Both do what they're told. And, obeying, they now face each other across the temple court.

Simeon sees them: a timid, awkward couple, the woman cradling a baby. He comes near, reaches out bony hands. Mary looks at Joseph. *Do you think it's all right?* He nods, and Mary lets the old man take her baby. His strength is surprising. And the moment the child is in his arms, song and prophecy spill forth—wonderful and terrible, hopeful and dreadful. A word to make a mother's heart surge, and then wilt. This child, Simeon declares, is the long-awaited One: Promise and Threat together, the rising and falling of many.

He hands the child back to the mother. She is silent with wonder. *This day is that day.*

Simeon smiles: *I have seen all I lived to see. Now dismiss your servant in peace.*

—m—

After my father died, my mother began to sort his personal belong-
ings. Some she kept. Some she discarded. And some she gave to us,
his three children. I got his Nikon camera and my brother got his Lynx
gold clubs and my sister got—honest—his pajamas. We each also
received little items, things that would have no value to anyone but us
(I suppose the pajamas fit this category): a stack of half-done cross-
word puzzle books; a boxful of wall plaques for achievement in the
corporate world of petroleum sales or for shooting closest to the pin
at some local golf tournament; his hat collection; a key chain I made
him in the eighth grade, his name stamped into the soft metal, the *h*
of *Buchanan* askew where the awl slipped.

And we got copies of letters he wrote my mother. One of them is
dated September 7, 1967. He would have been thirty-nine years old,
younger than I am now. He traveled a lot back then: sending his two-
tone tan and white Plymouth hurtling down long stretches of barren
road, cracked and uneven from frost-heaves, the odometer spinning
upward fast as the fruit on a slot machine. Eating another grease-
sodden hamburger alone again in another crowded smoky diner.
Sleeping on another swaybacked mattress alone again in another
musty roadside motel.

He wrote the letter from Grande Prairie, Alberta, up north where
prairie starts to pleat into tundra. The letterhead reads: "Stockdale
Motel, Doug & Betty Tosczak, Proprietors." I picture him in the small
square room, the smell of cigarette smoke thick in the carpet, the cur-

tains, the bedspread. It's nighttime. The window is a dark mirror, throwing back into the room a splintery rough-hewn image of itself. If you came into the room, you might notice the reflection of my father—the stark-edged outline, the black-shadowed hollows—before you noticed him. He sits at a small plain desk, his hand skittering, swift and deft, across the page, his writing, elegant as lacework, spinning out from the pen:

No doubt the mail has been the usual exciting assortment of overdue bills and Super-Valu flyers. I've lived so long in anticipation of something "breaking" for us, that if something ever did, my mind would break with it, and I would wind up my illustrious career cutting out paper dolls. The impetus of constant failure has propelled me to the verge of idiocy already. The knowledge of my educational and personal limitations has all but destroyed my self-confidence and has made me, I'm afraid, very negative....[36]

My father was a good man, though anger often sabotaged his best intentions. The anger, I see now, was fueled by chronic disappointment. He lived his life at the edge of heartbreak. But mostly now I remember my father's heroics: diving into a near-frozen lake in February to retrieve a fishing pole that my then ten-year-old sister had accidentally dropped in. He did it because she felt so bad about what she'd done, and he wanted to make it better. To console her.

I remember the friendship he made with an East Indian man. In those days, the early 1970s, Uganda's mad dictator Idi Amin, on one of his ruthless whims, evicted from his country thousands of East Indian landowners and shop owners. Most fled with only the clothes they wore. Many of them came to Canada. They were bureaucratically assigned in Ottawa to various places throughout the country. Ours was a northern mill town, redneck and hard-fisted, and the resentment among many of the locals toward the East Indians was deep and abiding.

One winter evening my father was driving home from work, trailing a public bus. The temperature was forty below zero, or colder. He could see, around the curve of road he was on, a man standing at the bus stop. He was rawboned and dark-skinned, dressed in a thin windbreaker, arms clutched tight around himself, shoulders thrust up to his jaw, shaking all over. He was in clear view. The bus driver sailed straight past him.

My dad stopped. He swung open the passenger door, invited the man to come in. The man was confused. My dad—holding up traffic—had to get out of his car and, with gestures and tone, convince the man to get into it. It took my dad another half-hour to negotiate past the unscalable barrier of language and figure out where the man lived. Thus began a friendship, which widened to include our family and his family. It took hold and lasted several years, until we moved away. They introduced us to curry. We helped them learn English.

My father was a good man. He was of earthly good. He sought to console others. Yet he never knew what would console himself. He likely wouldn't have known it had he held it in his arms.

That is the deep sadness in many people. They live toward something, yearn for it, strive for it—but never know quite what it is. They miss it deeply, woefully, sometimes with a sorrow like the sorrow we feel when we first realize our childhood is gone, irretrievable, forever. But still, they can't name what they miss. They can't tell you what it is, even if they held it in their arms. *I've lived so long in anticipation of something breaking for us that if something ever did, my mind would break with it.*

Simeon knew. He knew what would console him. He knew it when he saw it, when he held it in his arms. "That which was from the beginning, which we have heard, which we have seen with our eyes, which we have looked at and our hands have touched—this we proclaim" (1 John 1:1).

It is Christ. Christ was and is personal consolation. Seeing Him, Simeon could die in peace, satisfied. But Simeon's personal consolation was inextricably tied together with consolation for all. "The life appeared; we have seen it and testify to it, and we proclaim to you the eternal life, which was with the Father and has appeared to us.... And our fellowship is with the Father and with his Son, Jesus Christ. We write this to make our joy complete" (1 John 1:2–4). Simeon could die now because God's salvation for all people—for you, for your children, for your neighbors, even for your enemies—had appeared. He saw it and held it in his arms.

This was more than a private hope. It wasn't "Well, I can die a happy man, now that I've seen my children prosper, now that I've seen my children's children's children." This encounter with the Christ wasn't a personal windfall—like winning a lottery, like meeting a movie star—where his good fortune came at the expense of others, or excluded them. Simeon would not be consoled unless and until you are, too. He could not die happy unless and until you, and your children, and your children's children, are looked after too. Simeon's hope was intimate, but it was also epic, historic, cosmic. It was for him, and for you, and for me, and for all.

What is it that consoles you? What do you live for? What is the one thing that, knowing it is fulfilled, you could sing with Simeon the *Nunc Dimittis*—"Now dismiss your servant in peace"? When is your life's quest fulfilled? What would be enough?

Is the world enough? Is any one thing in it, or all things in it, enough?

Simeon's vision was high as the heavens, wide as the earth, deep as sheol. His hope was for here, for now, but not just: It was eternal and universal in scope. It was all-consuming and everlasting: To live was Christ; to die, gain.

Simeon never declares it directly, but everything else he says and does suggests that his hope in Christ was a resurrection hope. It was a heavenly one. Simeon, I think, would have understood the apostle Paul very well: "If only for this life we have hope in Christ, we are to be pitied more than all men" (1 Corinthians 15:19). He knew, as Paul so clearly did, that if all the Messiah's appearing meant was earthly gain, worldly conquest—Christ subduing arrogant Rome, purifying the sullied temple, reestablishing the ancient Davidic throne, restoring Israel's ruined glory, healing a few people along the way—well, that would be worth something, yes. That would be of some earthly good.

It would be some consolation.

It just wouldn't be enough. It wouldn't be salvation. It wouldn't make our joy complete. It wouldn't be the fullness of consolation.

Christ's appearance had to mean more.

And it did, and it does. It means that heaven and nature sing. It means peace on earth, to all men. It means salvation has appeared to all people. *"We proclaim to you the eternal life,* which was with the Father and has appeared to us" (1 John 1:2, emphasis added). It means we have all this, and heaven too.

Jesus has gone now to prepare a place for you; He's left you here to prepare for Him, by doing the works He sent you to do. By being of earthly good. One day, the Bridegroom will come back. He'll take you to be with Him, that you may be where He is (see John 14:1–4). He's made you heaven-bent.

That is consolation, more than you could ask or imagine.

Living for the Moment

I n the end she was cold, always cold. The coldness, to touch it, was as startling as some rough-skinned thing brushing your leg under the water. Or it was like a vast space opening out suddenly in the dark where you expected something solid—a floor, a wall, a ceiling. She was cold like that, and impossibly thin. Her thinness was like an optical illusion, a trick done with mirrors, a flaw in your own eye. She was a ghost only half-conjured. How could she be that thin and still have enough insides to hold together her outsides? Her body was a sharp-ridged topography of jutting bone, taut flesh, deep hollows, and one thing else: lumps, pressing up beneath her skin like fists.

Marlene was dying fast. Several months earlier, she'd gone to her doctor complaining of pain in hidden places, shortness of breath, an unshakable weariness. The doctor ordered tests. The diagnosis came back swift: lymphoma cancer. Inoperable. The cancer had begun in some secret depths, but now had latched itself on to anything, everything.

Marlene, her husband, Al, her grown children, her many grandchildren, her wide circle of friends, her church family—all were confident that she'd slip death this time. Marlene was still relatively young and abounding in good health. She would do what needed to be done: assume a routine of rest, therapy, diet, and stick with it. She and Al researched all the options, sifted them carefully, and blended together a regimen that would starve the death in her and feed the life.

And we prayed. We fasted. We gathered the elders and anointed her with oil. We held a prayer vigil for her. We laid hands on her in a special service for healing. Some friends took her to a faith healer in another city, and had the man pray for her.

We did it mostly because we could see little good in Marlene's dying, not now. We couldn't grasp how her death could be precious in the sight of God (see Psalm 116:15). Not now, not at this moment. She was a saint to us, a woman of such holy vigor and good solid sense, such cheerfulness and fervor, such clear-eyed conviction—she was of such earthly good—that we thought it best to petition God on those grounds: She's of more use to us right now than she is to You, God. Paul argued that way (see Philippians 1:20–26). And David did (see Psalm 30:9). None of us thought it wrong to imitate their example.

Marlene was a saint, but not a plaster-cast one. She had her blemishes. She probably spent too many hours involved in church committees, women's ministries, missionary support projects when her children were young and needed her to be with them. Both of them suffered, in different ways, because of it. And she had a certain crispness about her that, if you missed her heart, could be mistaken for haughtiness or impatience. She wielded her convictions with a formidable confidence that could silence all but the stoutest contender. Also, later in life, she and Al got involved in complex international business schemes that took him away for long stretches, strained their marriage, and ruined their finances.

But the core was solid. Like the apostle Paul, she at times appeared to be all things to all people. Indeed, Marlene had a kind of apostolic streak: it was she and Al whom God first inspired to plant the church in Duncan, and they worked as Paul must have, tireless, redoubtable, unswerving, tending it from seed to fruit. She was hospitable, an entertainer of angels, a friend to the lonely, the wounded, the perplexed, the sorrowful. The comfort she gave was more than sympathy. She exhorted. She strengthened feeble arms and steadied shaking knees with the Word—and with the example of her own unflinching, matter-of-fact faith. She was also a woman of prayer, and had the gift of administration: In the early years of our church, its fledgling existence perhaps was suspended between those two things.

Marlene was, above all, an evangelist. That was the fire in her bones. Every encounter was to her a divine appointment, an opportunity to show and, if needed, tell people about the love of God through Christ. God blessed her with extraordinary influence. The throng lining heaven's gateways to thank her will be huge, and larger than anyone on earth knows, for she did her work quietly, without trumpets blaring.

So we asked God to remove the cancer in Marlene. We wanted her to stay with us, among us, to do what few of us did, to inspire us to do it too.

But God said no. Against the rampart of her strictly-kept regimen, against the bulwark of traditional therapies, against the shields and weapons of our prayers, the cancer advanced without a single setback. It twined her bones and mounded up in thick tumors under her skin. It riddled her liver and studded her spleen. It filled her up, that cancer, and it emptied her out, winnowed her down to just a shadow.

And then, as it is with these things, we all knew at once: She was going to die. God was going to let Marlene die. At whatever high council these things are decided, the vote went against us. We were overruled, vetoed. There would be no appeal. It was finished.

Saintliness is seen as much, maybe more, in our death-style as in our lifestyle. Marlene rose to a new greatness in her dying. "She never once complained," her son, Kim, said. "She never felt sorry for herself. She never asked, 'Why me?' She never doubted God. She chose to bless others. I never saw my mother so thankful as in those final weeks. She was just thankful for—well, everything."

Her last days were spent in the hospital. Room 318. The local ministers call it the death chamber because it is reserved for those *in extremis,* in the last harrowing or oblivious moments of life. But for Marlene, it was sanctuary. A strange peace was in the place. Despite the massiveness of her cancer, she was without pain. She lay propped up against many pillows, tubes for oxygen and medicine streaming into her. Her family and some close friends were there, often silent—most words had worn out—though sometimes they sang one of her favorite hymns.

She had one last prayer: to see her newest grandchild before she died. Marlene's daughter Cindy—already with six children—was due, and tottered under the weight of it. But the baby slept on, serene inside his mother, and Marlene's life now was water cupped in the hand, running swiftly out. Then, that morning, the water broke. Not Marlene's. Cindy's. Her husband, Bob, brought her to the hospital and, one floor beneath where her mother lay dying, Cindy gave birth to little Eli. The nurses in attendance, at Cindy's urging, quickly swaddled the baby, placed mother and child in a wheelchair, and let Bob wheel them up a floor, to room 318. Marlene cradled Eli in her thin arms, and in her thin voice welcomed him to this world.

Now, sovereign Lord, dismiss Your servant in peace.

Somewhere in those last days, Marlene's friend Eugene (I tell his story on page 83) leaned close to her. He took her papery, willowy hand—her cold, cold hand—in his, and held it tight. Too tight. Marlene could barely turn her head, but she looked toward him. And then she spoke in a voice surprising in its clarity and strength. "It's all right, Gene. You can let go. Don't you understand? I've lived my entire life for this moment."

But one thing wasn't right.

Marlene had a regret. She brooded with a huge worry, wrestled with a taunting fear. It was about her husband, Al. She wasn't sure how he would manage without her. They had, for better or for worse, in sickness and in health, in riches and in want, been one flesh; her leaving was a rending of that, a tearing of him in half. She had always sorted him out, kept him disentangled from the sheer messiness of his own complex life. She felt her death a kind of betrayal or abandonment of him.

But her vow to him was "until death doth part us," and death would wait no longer. Al sat beside her. He held her hand. He didn't notice its coldness. He read her from Psalm 121: "I lift up my eyes to the hills—where does my help come from? My help comes from the LORD, the Maker of heaven and earth."

"Marlene," he said, "thank you for forty-five years of marriage."

He paused only a moment, and then spoke the words she longed to hear: "Run into the arms of Jesus."

Joy flooded her. In that single instant, youth came back to her: a brightness, a freshness, a wonder-struck expectancy that swept away her haggardness and pallor. Her body grew light. She sat up straight, jaunty, like a child waking after a good sound sleep. *I've lived my entire life for this moment.*

And she was gone.

Heaven-bent.

The publisher and author would love to hear your comments about this book. *Please contact us at:*
www.multnomah.net/buchanan

NOTES

1. J. R. R. Tolkien, "On Fairy Tales," cited in Philip Yancey, *The Jesus I Never Knew* (Grand Rapids, Mich.: Zondervan Publishing House, 1995), 218.

2. A. J. Conyers, *Eclipse of Heaven: The Loss of Transcendence and Its Effect on Modern Life* (South Bend, Ind.: St. Augustine Press, 1999).

3. C. S. Lewis, *Mere Christianity* (New York: Collier Books, 1960), 118.

4. Craig Brian Larson, ed., *Contemporary Illustrations for Preaching and Teaching* (Grand Rapids, Mich.: Baker Books, 1996), 102.

5. Marshall Shelley, "Two Minutes to Eternity," *Christianity Today*, 16 May 1994, 25–7.

6. Dr. Irvin D. Yalom, *The Theory and Practice of Group Psychotherapy*, 4th ed. (New York: Basic Books, 1995), cited in Richard John Neuhaus, *Death on a Friday Afternoon: Meditations on the Last Words of Jesus from the Cross* (New York: Basic Books, 2000), 253.

7. Mark Buchanan, "Trapped in the Cult of the Thing," *Christianity Today*, 6 September 1999, 62–71.

8. George Herbert, "The Pulley," *The Norton Anthology of English Literature*, 4th ed. (New York: W.W. Norton & Co., 1979), 1:1336.

9. Lewis, *Mere Christianity*, 119.

10. Mark Twain, *The Adventures of Huckleberry Finn* (New York: Fawcett Columbine, 1996), 5–6.

11. Daniel A. Brown, *What the Bible Reveals About Heaven* (Ventura, Calif.: Regal, 1999), 188.

12. We can, of course, think of exceptions. Would anyone value the last mosquito or toothache? And some things on earth—love, sunshine, chocolate—suffer no diminishment in value with increase.

13 Of course the word more makes sense only on a scale of comparison. I don't think we can escape, even in heaven, all scales of comparison. Even there, things are more or less, higher or lower, bigger or smaller. What I think is eliminated, or at least radically reordered, is the scale of comparison in values—the categories of better and worse.

14. Cited in Joni Eareckson Tada, *Heaven: Your Real Home* (Grand Rapids, Mich.: Zondervan, 1995), 89.

15. Back page of *Maclean's*, 24 September 2001.

16. Helen Keller in John MacArthur, *God: Coming Face-to-Face with His Majesty* (Wheaton, Ill.: Victor Books, 1993), 95.

17. Billy Graham, as quoted in *Christianity Today*, 12 September 1977, 19.

18. Tom Wright, *For All God's Worth: True Worship and the Calling of the Church* (Grand Rapids, Mich.: Eerdmans, 1997), 10–1.

19. Adapted from a joke from Jerry Newman, e-mail, 28 March 2001.

20. Os Guinness, *The Call: Finding and Fulfilling the Central Purpose of Your Life* (Nashville, Tenn.: Word, 1998), 106.

21. The same miracles that brought many to place their hope and trust in Jesus Christ brought others to resent, fear, and despise Him. A key example is the raising of Lazarus from the dead. Many saw and believed. But others saw and, though not denying the miracle, were so threatened by it that they plotted how to kill Jesus. See John 11:45–48.

22. Charles Spurgeon, *The Quotable Spurgeon* (Wheaton, Ill.: Harold Shaw Publishers, Inc., 1990), 62.

23. Philip Yancey, "What's Heaven For?" *Christianity Today,* 26 October 1998, 104.

24. Gary Nelson, Edmonton Pastors' Conference, 27 February 2001.

25. This illustration was suggested to me by A. J. Conyers, *Eclipse of Heaven: The Loss of Transcendence and Its Effect on Modern Life* (South Bend, Ind.: St. Augustine Press, 1991).

26. BBC Ministries, *Our Daily Bread* (Monday, 4 October 1997).

27. J. R. R. Tolkien, *The Lord of the Rings,* Book 1 (London: Unwin Paperbacks, 1966), 168–9.

28. Aldous Huxley, *Brave New World* (London: Grafton Books, 1977), 46.

29. Idea from Harry Blamires, "The Eternal Weight of Glory," *Christianity Today,* 27 May 1991, 32.

30. Richard Adams, *Watership Down* (Harmondsworth, Middlesex, England: Penguin Books, 1977), 287.

31. Walker Percy, *The Thanatos Syndrome* (New York: Ivy Books, 1987).

32. Margaret Kim Peterson, "A Good Death," *Christianity Today,* 22 May 2000, 64–9. Peterson refuses to explain how her husband contracted AIDS, because she says it's too easy then to render judgment about his moral innocence or guilt in a way that clouds rather than clarifies the meaning of his death.

33. Timothy Jones, "Death in the Mirror," *Christianity Today,* 24 June 1991, 30.

34. Ibid.

35. Lorna Chao, "Testimony for Miss Kathy Merill's Memorial Service," 7 April 2000.

36. Bruce A. Buchanan, personal letter to "Dear Adorable Wifie, Loquacious Children, Incorrigible Dog, Indolent Cats," 7 September 1967.

ACKNOWLEDGMENTS

Of all the illusions we cherish, perhaps the most enduring is the myth of self-reliance: that we make ourselves, or make anything by ourselves. The truth is that each of our lives is woven so intricately and intimately with the lives of others that one strand plucked out could unravel the whole. I wear clothes, drive a car, type on a computer, eat food—each made available to me because of someone else's industry, time, skill.

Most of these people I will never know: the woman who stitched my shirt, or the man who spun the cloth from which it was cut; the farmer who seeded the soil and grew the grain that was ground into flour and sold to a bakery; the baker who blended that flour with a half-dozen other things—each with its own rich history—and who baked it in an oven wrought by people who work with wires and bricks and metal; the driver who carried what the baker made to the store near my home; the clerk who stocked it on the shelf; the cashier who rang it through. On and on it goes, a vast skein of dependencies and contingencies, of gathering and scattering, of each of us needing the other.

This book is like that. On the cover, it bears my name—bold, emblazoned, solitary. As if I wrote it all on my own. As if no other minds, no other hands, no other souls poured anything into it. But that's an illusion. This book is the work of a vast company of people: pilgrims and poets, tinkers and tradesmen, theologians and saints, the living and the dead. These closing pages are my meager effort to thank a few.

The people at Multnomah have become my friends. You have shown kindness to and support for my family and me that goes far beyond mere business—you have gathered us into your community. I thank especially: my editor, Judith St. Pierre, who understands how finicky and feisty a writer can be about commas. Judith, you and I know that whole worlds hinge on them. Don Jacobson, that gentle giant, whose example of humility and boldness inspires us all. And Bill and Sheila Jensen and family. Bill, you have taught me that heaven must be very much like fishing the Deschutes River in steelhead season, or like a tenor's well-sung aria as he mimics his death throes.

I am grateful to Ann Spangler, my agent, for her earthy humor and heavenly wisdom. Once again, Ann, you have shepherded me through the strange land of book-making and book-selling, and brought me through to the other side without any noticeable scars or bruises.

I thank my church family, who over the past six years have walked with me the narrow road between being heavenly-minded and of earthly good. I love being on the journey with you. Thanks especially to Joy Brewtser for taking the time to read through and make comments on the manuscript—and on your holiday, yet! Your counsel was excellent, as always, and I heeded it, though you are innocent of any of the book's remaining flaws.

I thank my family—Cheryl, my wife, and Adam, Sarah, and Nicola, our children—each and all of whom radiate the light of forever for me. You have never withdrawn your loving presence, even in my many absences, as I holed up, hobbitlike, for yet another day of writing. I am glad, for Christ's sake, to be heaven-bent, but that we are heaven-bent together fills me with joy unspeakable.

All glory and praise I give to my Lord Jesus Christ, the author and perfecter of my faith. In You I live and move and have my being. Through You I have the hope of glory, the delight of Things Unseen. May it grow ever brighter and stronger, from this day until *That Day*, when I see You face-to-face.

Shalom,

Mark